MAKING VIDEO GAMES

Essential Library
An Imprint of Abdo Publishing
abdobooks.com

BY TOM STREISSGUTH

abdobooks.com

Printed in the United States of America, North Mankato, Minnesota.
052024
092024

THIS BOOK CONTAINS
RECYCLED MATERIALS

Cover Photos: Anton Gvozdikov/Shutterstock Images, cover (VR headset); Roman Arbuzov/Shutterstock Images, cover (controller); Shutterstock Images, cover (background); Yuliia Konakhovska/Shutterstock Images, cover (hearts)
Interior Photos: Shutterstock Images, 1 (background), 65, 74, 86, 100; Yuliia Konakhovska/Shutterstock Images, 1 (hearts); izusek/E+/Getty Images, 4; Ian Dagnall Computing/Alamy, 7; Jeff Chiu/AP Images, 8; Marbella Studio/Shutterstock Images, 11; Nicolas Maeterlinck/Belga Mag/AFP/Getty Images, 12; Volker Steger/Science Source, 16; Interfoto/History/Alamy, 19; Sankei Archive/Getty Images, 23; David McNew/Getty Images News/Getty Images, 24; Richard Levine/Alamy, 26; Game Developers Conference, 27; Lluis Gene/AFP/Getty Images, 28; Joe Scarnici/WireImage/Getty Images, 31; Francisco Kjolseth/The Salt Lake Tribune/AP Images, 34; Colleen Michaels/Alamy, 37; Allison Dinner/AP Images, 38; Duffy-Marie Arnoult/WireImage/Getty Images, 41; The Asahi Shimbun/Getty Images, 42; Andia/Universal Images Group/Getty Images, 45; Christophe Archambault/AFP/Getty Images, 46, 91; Justin Sullivan/Getty Images News/Getty Images, 50; Zety Akhzar/Shutterstock Images, 52; Pierrick Villette/Abaca Press/Sipa USA/AP Images, 56–57; Natallia Hryharenka/Shutterstock Images, 59; Christian Petersen/Getty Images News/Getty Images, 60; Rob Monk/Edge Magazine/Future/Getty Images, 62; M4OS Photos/Alamy, 66; Ugo Amez/Sipa/AP Images, 68–69; Chesnot/Getty Images Entertainment/Getty Images, 73, 79; Alistair Berg/DigitalVision/Getty Images, 76; Amlan Mathur/Alamy, 82; Costfoto/NurPhoto/Getty Images, 88; Nano Calvo/VW Pics/Universal Images Group/Getty Images, 93; PG/Bauer-Griffin/GC Images/Getty Images, 96–97; John Keeble/Getty Images News/Getty Images, 99; Andrew Boydston/Shutterstock Images, 101

Editor: Laura Stickney
Series Designer: Maggie Villaume

Library of Congress Control Number: 2023949560

Publisher's Cataloging-in-Publication Data
Names: Streissguth, Tom, author.
Title: Making video games / by Tom Streissguth
Description: Minneapolis, Minnesota: Abdo Publishing, 2025 | Series: Making media | Includes online resources and index.
Identifiers: ISBN 9781098293383 (lib. bdg.) | ISBN 9798384912651 (ebook)
Subjects: LCSH: Video game designers--Juvenile literature. | Video games--Software--Juvenile literature. | Video games--Programming--Juvenile literature. | Video games industry--Juvenile literature. | Video game music--Juvenile literature.
Classification: DDC 794.8--dc23

CONTENTS

CHAPTER ONE

VIDEO GAME ASSIGNMENT

It was the first school day of the new year. Dana strolled down the crowded hall to her first class, computer science. She knew it was going to be a big day.

Mr. Hawthorne would be handing out the project assignment for the semester. Everyone in the class would have to design a video game. They could choose to make a personal computer (PC) game or a mobile game. They could pick which game engine to use. And they could make any kind of game they wanted. There was only one rule for the assignment: the game had to have one fully playable level.

DESIGNING A GAME

The first step in creating a game was choosing a platform. Dana picked a mobile platform because it involved a smaller screen and simpler controls. Her game would run on the iOS operating system, which is used on iPhones. There were plenty of online tutorials for coders and game developers. Several game engines were also

Young people interested in developing video games can participate in computer science programs or use online learning resources. Some high schools and colleges also offer game development classes.

GAME GENRES

Most video games fall into common categories called genres. These genres often have names shortened to acronyms. Some games are first-person shooter (FPS) games. In FPS games, gamers see a three-dimensional world through the eyes of the player character. They may shoot enemies or explore different environments. Another type of game is a role-playing game (RPG). In an RPG, a gamer plays as a character that develops over time, gaining more power, learning new skills, and finding gear such as weapons and armor. In real-time strategy (RTS) games, players command armies from a bird's-eye view. In a massively multiplayer online (MMO) game, thousands of players inhabit an online world. They work together or compete to defeat enemies and complete quests.

available for iOS. Some were freely available online. Dana picked Unity, a game engine Mr. Hawthorne had suggested.

The next step was putting together the game design document. Dana needed to create a document that explained what her game was. She had to include the game's genre, how the gameplay worked, and how players progressed through the game.

First, Dana wrote down classic games she enjoyed playing. Then she got into the details. Her game would start as a simple match-three game. A match-three game features a grid of icons, such as the ones that appear in the mobile game *Candy Crush*. Players line up three icons in a row. When that happens, the icons explode and new ones appear in their places. If players line up four or more icons in a row, they earn more points. The basic code for a match-three game was built into the Unity software. All Dana had to do was use the program's menus to customize the gameplay for her own needs.

Dana created a 17-by-17 match-three grid. For the icons, she decided to use pictures of her classmates. She had a card with all her classmates' pictures on it. After picture day, the

Like other match-three mobile games, *Candy Crush* features colorful designs, addictive gameplay, and levels that get progressively harder. Since launching, the game has been downloaded more than three billion times.

IMAGINE — CREATE — GROW
DO MORE WITH UNITY
Unity
Unity®
MADE WITH UNITY SHOWCASE
Unity®

photographer had included these cards in the photo envelopes. Dana used a scanner to turn the physical pictures into a digital file. Then she used image editing software to split each person's photo into a separate image. These images became icons in the match-three grid.

Dana liked when games let players customize the gameplay. So she allowed players to upload their own pictures into her game too. They could then replace the icons with pictures of friends, rock stars, celebrities, or pets.

Next Dana thought about what else to add to the game. She decided that if players scored enough points, they would progress to a side-scrolling snowboarding game. Dana modeled it on one of her favorite mobile games, *Alto's Odyssey*. In the game, a little sprite—a figure built from pixels—jumped, rolled, and flipped in a two-dimensional environment. The figure bounced off balloons and jumped over chasms.

Dana discovered that the code for this game mechanic was available in the Unity engine. She studied the engine's preset code and made a few changes to it. She also created sprites for a dozen different characters the player could choose from. She liked when games had a variety of sprites.

PLATFORMER GAMES

First-time game developers often begin by picking a genre for their games. Many choose platformer games. In these games, a character navigates through two-dimensional levels, jumping between platforms and over gaps. Enemies may appear to fight the player or block them from progressing. Platformer games have relatively simple gameplay compared with other genres. This makes them a good fit for new developers. Still, developers need to be creative to set their platformer game apart from the rest.

Video game developers can learn more about game engines at events such as the Game Developers Conference (GDC). At GDC 2023, Unity showcased its latest technology and games people made using the engine.

Dana tinkered with her game's design for hours. She tried to get the figures and landscape just right. She also created some funny non-player characters (NPCs), including mixed martial arts penguins, schoolyard bully whales, and rapping dodo birds.

Dana also experimented with character movements in the game. She made it possible for characters in the game to do impossible wall runs and ceiling walks. There were crazy leaps down mountainsides and on top of trains. Working with the presets available in the game engine, Dana even added a spiderweb-assisted vaulting move.

FINISHING TOUCHES

Now Dana could add details to her game. No story or dialogue were necessary, but she still needed to add sound effects. Dana used her phone to record some sound effects in her bedroom. She shook a bag of keys to make the sound of breaking glass. She clicked a briefcase latch to make the sound that would play when icons were cleared from the match-three grid. Dana recorded the effects on her phone and then used a computer program to convert the short recordings into WAV files. The game would play these sound files at the appropriate times during gameplay.

One of Dana's classmates told her about a website that offered free sound effects. Dana went to the site and downloaded sounds for various parts of the game, such as winning a level and selecting options on the main menu. Dana also needed

Some video game designers use graphic design tools to create characters, settings, and other game elements.

a soundtrack. She found a website with free available music and picked a mix of tracks ranging from K-pop tunes to twangy country songs. The music was meant to be funny and unpredictable.

Once Dana had added these elements to her game, she took another look at the assignment guidelines. Mr. Hawthorne wanted students to submit a two-page marketing plan for their game. In the plan, Dana needed to answer some questions. Who was the audience for her game? What did the competition look like? What platform should she use? Would the game be free to play or subscription based? These were important things game developers needed to consider when creating a game. Dana thought hard about these questions as she made her marketing plan.

010
RESIDENTIAL QUARTERS
You have no clue how much time has passed, but when you awaken the man is gone and strangely enough, none of your stuff is.
1) "What happened?"
AOC

As the semester went by, the deadline for Dana's game project was coming up faster than a gate on her snowboarding slalom course. Dana wished time could slow down. Testing a game to find bugs and errors took time. Sometimes her game would freeze at the end of the match-three part. The snowboarding gameplay slowed to a crawl when too much was happening on-screen. The on-screen text had spelling errors too. Dana tracked down the issues and fixed the code.

STARTING OUT WITH MODS

Developing a video game is a big task. One way to learn the complicated skills required for game development is by creating mods, or modifications. These are changes to levels, characters, or gameplay in an existing game. Many professional game developers started by making mods. They shared their mods on the internet. Feedback from friends and strangers helped them figure out what they were doing right and wrong.

THE FINAL PRODUCT

Finally the last day of class came. It was time for Dana to turn in her game. But after all this time, she didn't have a title for it. She had been so focused on the gameplay, levels, and music that she hadn't bothered to choose a name.

She needed a catchy, memorable title. After brainstorming for a while, Dana came up with the perfect name. Her very first video game would be called *Super Skater Sprites.*

Mr. Hawthorne promised to submit grades on the games in a week. He had to test 24 different games created by teenage amateurs. *Poor guy,* Dana thought. *He'll probably go insane by the time he's done.*

Game developers must consider several factors when designing and testing a game. These may include sound design, the simplicity of the controls, and whether the game's look and theme will appeal to players.

A week later, Mr. Hawthorne uploaded the project grades. Dana was anxious to read her teacher's reaction. She knew Mr. Hawthorne was a tough grader. A feeling of dread had been settling over her all week. But when Dana scrolled through the feedback on her project, it wasn't so bad. Mr. Hawthorne had given her a B. She read through his feedback.

"Lots of energy and original content here," wrote Mr. Hawthorne. "But your choice of two completely different environments doesn't work. Gamers want to be absorbed by their games. They want to get into a unique feeling and style, because they might be there for many hours. When you change up the gameplay, you break the spell. The gamer has to adjust. It's like having to master a new game. It's distracting and feels wrong. Remember the assignment: *one* playable level."

> **"It should be the experience that is touching. What I strive for is to make the person playing the game the director. All I do is help them feel that, by playing, they're creating something that only they could create.[1]"**
>
> ***—Shigeru Miyamoto, Nintendo game developer***

As Dana read this feedback, she got a sinking feeling. She wished she had paid a little more attention to the guidelines when she started working on the project. She made the same mistake whenever she played video games, always rushing into the action before finishing the tutorials.

Dana continued reading her teacher's feedback. "If you had been working for a real game company, game reviewers would probably have identified the same issues I did," explained Mr. Hawthorne. "They might have given *Super Skater Sprites* a low review score, which would result in low sales. But you learned the engine and came up with some fun stuff on the way. No crashes or glitches, either. Nice work!"

Dana wasn't crushed after reading her teacher's feedback, but she did feel a little mad at first. All that time and work for a B? But after reading through Mr. Hawthorne's notes a few more times, Dana decided he was probably right. In coming up with the concept, Dana had used games that she liked, partly so she could have fun building the game. This might have been the wrong move. Game designers had to make games fun for the gamer, not themselves. In the process of learning the skills and tools required to build the game, Dana hadn't thought enough about the gamer's experience.

Dana decided she'd keep designing games. Her next one would be even better. But next time, she'd get out of her room and out of her comfort zone. She'd work on improving her game design skills. She would find people to play and test the game. And she would listen carefully to what they had to say about it. By following these steps, Dana hoped to become a stronger game developer—and someday, maybe even a professional one.

CHAPTER TWO

THE HISTORY OF VIDEO GAMES

The first video games were created on big, boxy computing machines called mainframes. In 1962, Steve Russell was a student at the Massachusetts Institute of Technology (MIT). He wanted to create a space combat simulation. He programmed a game called *Spacewar!* for MIT's PDP-1 computer.

Russell built control boxes topped with switches. Two players used the boxes to maneuver their ships around a circular screen. The ships aimed and fired while circling a star, whose gravity drew the ships toward it. If the ships were hit, they exploded.

The game program, like other computer software of the time, was recorded on paper tape. A series of punches in the paper transmitted instructions to the machine. This made it possible to install *Spacewar!* on other computers. The game quickly spread as colleges across the country purchased PDP-1s for their computer labs.

At the Computer History Museum in Mountain View, California, visitors can see a working PDP-1 computer. *Spacewar!* made this type of computer famous.

Spacewar! attracted the attention of other game creators. Nolan Bushnell, a student at the University of Utah, believed a game like *Spacewar!* could be a big hit with the public. In 1971, he programmed the first commercial arcade game, *Computer Space*. The game came in a tall cabinet with a screen on top and controls in the center. It was manufactured by Nutting Associates, a California electronics company.

THE *PONG* CRAZE

In 1972, the Magnavox company released the Odyssey, the first game console made for home use. The Odyssey stored games on cartridges. Gamers inserted the cartridges into the console and played using two knob controllers. The gameplay appeared on a television screen.

Around the same time, Bushnell founded Atari Inc. to make more games. In September 1972, Atari employee Allan Alcorn finished programming *Pong*, the company's first product. It was a tennis game in which players bounced a small blip back and forth across the screen. The game ran on computer circuits in a cabinet, and it displayed on a black-and-white screen. Bushnell brought a prototype unit to Andy Capp's Tavern, a small bar in Sunnyvale, California. The game cabinet was placed near pinball machines.

SPACEWAR! MASTER

At the Computer History Museum in Mountain View, California, visitors can play *Spacewar!* on an original PDP-1 machine. Steve Russell, the game's programmer, volunteered at the museum. He played *Spacewar!* matches against anyone who challenged him. Russell rarely lost, even when he played against professional gamers who had trained for weeks.

The original Magnavox Odyssey gaming system came with 12 games. They were simple two-player games, such as table tennis and volleyball.

Customers at Andy Capp's Tavern soon lined up to play *Pong*. Atari set up an assembly line in a former roller-skating rink to manufacture more cabinets. Over the next few years, the company sold thousands of *Pong* units across the country. Imitators began trying to cash in on a new mania for video arcade games. Video games took over the arcade space. Pinball machines and other old gaming devices became less popular.

In 1977, Atari released the Atari Video Computer System (VCS). This home gaming console later became known as the Atari 2600. Some of its games were home versions of hit arcade games such as *Pong* and *Space Invaders*. But others were original releases, including *Adventure* and *Pitfall!* The Atari 2600 was much more successful than the earlier Magnavox Odyssey. It created a big market for home video games.

PLAYING THE CLASSICS

Video game nostalgia has swept the game market for a long time. Old games are reengineered for new systems, while arcade players still drop quarters into antique cabinets offering old games such as *Donkey Kong, Pac-Man,* or *Asteroids*. Playing the classics allows aging gamers to relive times when game technology was brand-new. The pull is so strong that some players become experts in old games. There's even an esports tournament for nostalgia players. The Retro World Series features games on the Atari 2600, Nintendo Entertainment System, Sega Genesis, and other early systems.

CRASH AND RECOVERY

Atari and other video game companies thrived in the late 1970s and early 1980s. But by 1983, the US video game industry was experiencing a major crash. Too many consoles and low-quality games were available.

E.T. the Extra-Terrestrial for the Atari 2600 is one famous example. The game was based on the 1982 movie of the same name, and Atari wanted it in stores for Christmas 1982. The company gave a single programmer just five weeks to make the game from scratch.[1] It was a sales failure and is commonly cited as one of the worst games ever made. Across the industry, sales plummeted, and some people wondered if video games were simply a passing trend.

In the mid-1980s, the Japanese company Nintendo helped revive the game industry. Nintendo started out in 1889 making playing cards. It branched into video games in the 1980s. In 1983, Nintendo released a home console, the Famicom, in Japan. Two years later, the console was released in the United States. It was called the Nintendo Entertainment System (NES).

With games such as *Super Mario Bros.* and *The Legend of Zelda*, the NES became a massive success around the world and showed that video games had lasting appeal. Nintendo's handheld console, the Game Boy, arrived in 1989. Its next-generation home console, the Super NES, hit stores in 1990.

> **"I calculated it out once that I had produced game code (finished, debugged, and documented) at 13 times the industry average! . . . For the time I had, and given the problem I had to solve, I think I did a pretty good job with it.[2]"**
>
> ***—Howard Scott Warshaw, developer of* E.T. the Extra-Terrestrial *for the Atari 2600***

Each new generation of game consoles was more sophisticated than the last. New games featured sharper graphics, clearer sound, and more complex gameplay. This meant making a game took more work. Early releases on the Atari 2600 could be made by just one person. The Super NES game *Super Mario World* required a team of six programmers, who were each assigned a game element. For example, one programmer was responsible for Mario's movement and actions.[3]

NEW PLAYERS IN THE GAME INDUSTRY

In 1994, Japanese company Sony introduced its first game console, the PlayStation. Most earlier consoles used cartridges to store games. But PlayStation games used compact discs (CDs). These discs had much more storage capacity than cartridges. This allowed developers to create more sprawling adventures than ever before. As games grew bigger, so did the teams required to make them. *Final Fantasy VII*, a role-playing game (RPG) that spanned three CDs, involved more than 150 people.[4]

The industry's growth led to new game companies, including Activision, Electronic Arts, and Epic Games. These third-party developers created games for other companies' game consoles. Jobs in the industry also became more specialized. Writers, game designers, artists, programmers, voice performers, and other specialists found roles in the industry.

To fund a game, developers usually partnered with publishers. The publisher agreed to manufacture, package, promote, and distribute the game. Both the developer and publisher earned money from sales. Some companies, including Activision and Electronic Arts, worked as both publishers and developers.

In the late 1990s, computer software company Microsoft created the Xbox. It released the first version of this console to the North American market in late 2001. Microsoft CEO Bill Gates knew his system had to make a big splash. If the company couldn't come up with a hit game, established companies such as Nintendo and Sony would crush the Xbox.

Microsoft purchased the game studio Bungie, which made the first-person

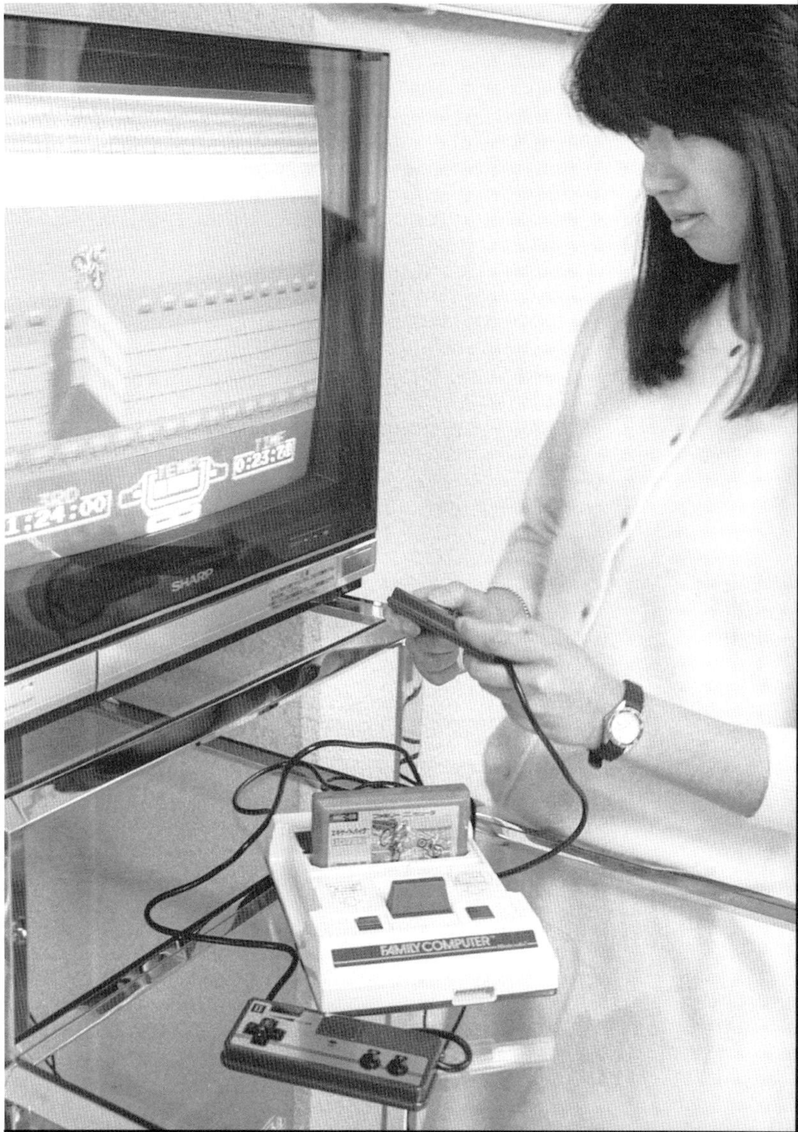

Nintendo's original Famicom featured two controllers connected to the sides of the game console by cords. Games came on plastic cartridges that were inserted into the console.

In November 2001, Bill Gates, *right*, and his colleague Seamus Blackley, *left*, demonstrated the Xbox at the COMDEX computer and technology trade show.

shooter (FPS) game *Halo: Combat Evolved*. Available exclusively for the Xbox, the game became a critical and commercial success. It helped the Xbox succeed and became a major franchise for Microsoft. Hiring talented development teams has been a way for large companies to gain a competitive advantage.

With the Xbox, Microsoft pioneered online console gaming. PC players had been playing online for years. But online gaming went mainstream after Microsoft introduced its Xbox Live subscription service in 2002. Players could create friend lists, join games online, and chat through headsets. Development teams grew to handle these new features, and the cost of making modern games grew too. In 2004, *Halo 2* arrived for the Xbox. Bungie needed three years, 190 people, and $40 million to make the game.[5]

THE MODERN GAME INDUSTRY

With modern game consoles and computers, games have more complex graphics, sound, and gameplay than ever before. The production of the biggest, most high-profile releases, known as AAA games, can be expensive. The 2022 installment of the *Call of Duty* FPS franchise, *Call of Duty: Modern Warfare II*, cost up to $300 million to make.[6] The game was published by Activision and developed by Infinity Ward, with support from ten additional game development studios.[7] It took fewer programmers to make *Super Mario World* three decades earlier than it took studios to make a *Call of Duty* game.

For many in the industry, this cost has made game development unsustainable. In an internal email released as part of a court case in 2023, Xbox head Phil Spencer discussed the challenge. He wrote, "Very few companies can afford to spend the $200M an Activision or Take 2 spend to put a title like *Call of Duty* or *Red Dead Redemption* on the shelf. . . . AAA publishers

GAME ENGINES

Modern developers can use several game engines. Two of the most popular are Unreal Engine and Unity. Unreal Engine is made by Epic Games, the creators of *Fortnite*. However, its origins go back much further than *Fortnite*. Unreal Engine dates back to 1998. New versions have added more features over the years. Unreal Engine 5 arrived in 2022, bringing advanced new graphics technologies. Unity is made by Unity Technologies and was first available in 2005. It is a popular choice for developing mobile games.

High-profile game releases often involve big marketing campaigns. In 2022, billboards advertising *Call of Duty: Modern Warfare II* were displayed in New York City's Times Square.

are milking their top franchises but struggling to refill their portfolio of hit franchises. Most AAA publishers are riding the success of franchises created 10+ years ago."[8]

But some developers are taking a different path. Independent games flourished in the 2010s and 2020s. Inexpensive development tools and new digital distribution methods have made it easy for any developer to create a hit game. Some big independent releases were made by a single person. *Stardew Valley* is the work of Eric Barone, and *Undertale* was made by Toby Fox. Mobile games have also become easier to make. These successes show there are multiple ways to make an impact in the modern game industry.

DAISUKE AMAYA

In 1999, Daisuke "Pixel" Amaya was a student at a Japanese university. Like many technology nerds, he loved video games. His favorite kind was the old-fashioned 2D platformer game, where players ran, jumped, and blasted things. Amaya wanted to work in the world of video games, but he also knew there wouldn't be many jobs in the field after he graduated.

Amaya didn't care. He decided getting a job in games wasn't as important as making games. So he started working on his own game. Without a boss or company calling the shots, Amaya was free to make a game he loved.

To learn how to make video games, Amaya studied books and websites. He even created his own game engine. He worked a regular job and spent his free time working on the game. Amaya used the classic platformer games *Metroid* and *Blaster Master* as models. He designed his game's main character, Quote, and built 12 side-scrolling levels.

Amaya also wrote the game's story and music. He titled the game *Cave Story*. After five years, the game was ready. It sparked a wave of independent game production.

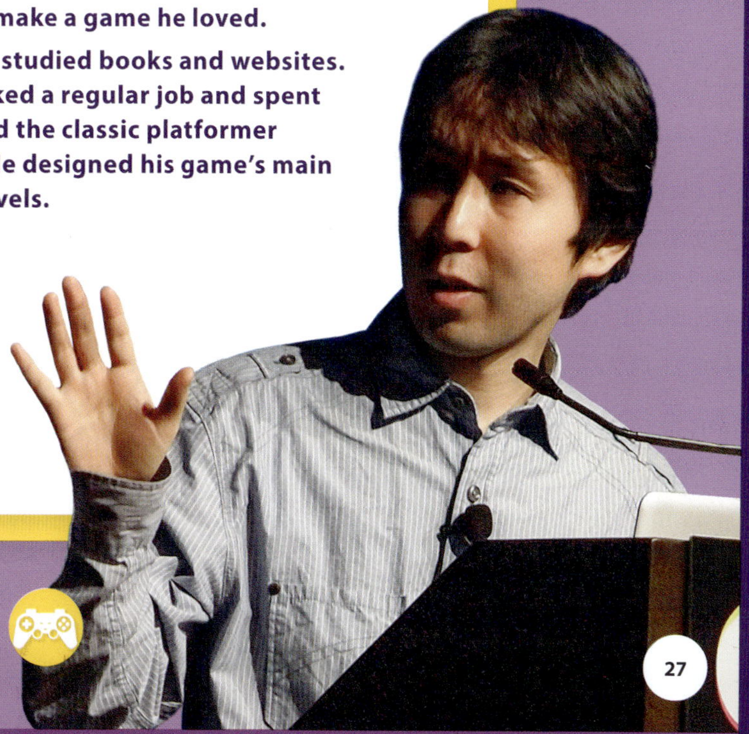

Amaya discussed the process of creating *Cave Story* at the 2011 Game Developers Conference.

SAMSUNG
SAMSUNG
SAMSUNG
GIGABYTE
P8H77-M

CHAPTER **THREE**

PREPRODUCTION FOR PROFESSIONAL GAMES

Before a professional game development company makes a video game, someone must come up with an idea. Most developers have a pipeline of game ideas created by their own employees. A creative director and staff keep the pipeline moving by making decisions. This might include rejecting the game, offering it to another developer, or keeping the idea and creating a prototype. Most game companies rarely accept game ideas sent in by outside individuals.

The original concept is the seed from which the game will grow. The game's creator sets up the concept in a document. At this stage, a video game is not yet a project under active development. It's just a written proposal that explains the game's story, genre, and characters. The proposal may also identify the game's intended audience and estimate its development schedule and budget.

Once a game proposal is ready, it becomes a pitch. This is a request for investment. The creator submits the pitch to a publisher, who will consider the

Many professional game developers make games based on popular franchises. French developer Gameloft, for example, made a mobile game featuring the minion characters from the *Despicable Me* movies.

FIRST PARTY, SECOND PARTY, THIRD PARTY

In the game industry, the terms *first party, second party,* and *third party* refer to how game developers relate to the companies that make consoles and publish their games. Some big game studios are part of larger corporations. These first-party developers include Naughty Dog, which is owned by Sony. Retro Studios is a part of Nintendo, and Obsidian Entertainment is a part of Xbox Game Studios. Second-party developers aren't owned by another company, but they release games exclusively for a single console. Game Freak, for example, creates Pokémon games for Nintendo. Third-party developers work independently on their own games and can release them for any console. Ubisoft and Electronic Arts are among the biggest third-party developers.

game's potential. If a game is part of a popular series or based on a successful movie franchise, the publisher might believe the game will be a big seller. It may offer a large budget. If the publisher thinks the game will appeal to a narrower audience, it will approve a smaller budget. If the publisher wants to move forward with a game, it signs a contract with the developer.

STAFFING UP

When a professional game developer schedules a new project, the preproduction process begins. The developer must put together a team and decide who will be doing which tasks. Developers usually hire people who know how to use game engines and code in different programming languages. Prior experience with game development helps, as does a college degree in software engineering or a related field.

In the early days of video game development, a single person could program a game. This person created the art, characters, and gameplay on their own. The process usually took no more than a few months.

AMY HENNIG

Amy Hennig studied English literature at the University of California. Later, she attended film school in San Francisco, California. Hennig's specialty was visual narrative. This is the art of making characters, telling stories, and making everything look good.

These skills led Hennig to a freelance job with Atari. She worked as an artist on *Electrocop,* which was released in 1989. Her early experience in the video game industry convinced her that games could rival film as a creative medium. Hennig dropped her plans for a film career and joined Electronic Arts in 1991.

After moving to game developer Crystal Dynamics, Hennig wrote and designed the *Legacy of Kain* series, a popular dark fantasy adventure franchise, in the late 1990s. Later, she created the game *Uncharted* at the developer Naughty Dog. This blockbuster adventure game inspired several sequels and eventually a movie adaptation starring Mark Wahlberg and Tom Holland.

Hennig started her own game development studio, Skydance New Media, in 2019. She worked with Lucasfilm on a new *Star Wars* game. She also contributed to *Forspoken,* a 2023 open-world fantasy and exploration game, as a writer and creative consultant.

At the 2012 Writers Guild Awards, Hennig won the award for Outstanding Achievement in Videogame Writing for the game *Uncharted 3: Drake's Deception*.

But today it takes hundreds of people to make most video games. A project manager organizes teams to work on various aspects of the project. For example, one team might create 3D models for characters, backgrounds, and weapons. Another team might design the layout of the levels. There may be teams for coding, sound design, and even creating the game's menus. During preproduction, the developer must make an important choice by deciding which engine the game will use. The company may license an engine, such as Unity, or use its own engine in-house.

> **"Preproduction must be allowed to be a chaotic process. You can't plan when inspiration will strike and you can't schedule the date when you'll have worked out all your seemingly intractable problems.[2]"**
>
> ***—Mark Cerny, game developer, 2002***

During preproduction, a game developer must also prepare for any bumps in the long road to the game's release date. Over the months or years it takes to complete a video game, the roles assigned to people may change. Problems may come up during the development process. New hires may join the developer, and some staff members may resign. There may be a lot of money on the line. The budget for AAA games can be more than $100 million.[1] This means it's important for developers to plan ahead and prepare for obstacles.

For this reason, many developers hire freelancers and remote workers who are available to help when needed.

Using freelancers helps developers control costs. Full-time staff members are paid a salary for as long as it takes to complete the project, but freelancers are simply paid a fee. The fee is due when a project is complete or a milestone is achieved.

A computer designer specializing in character animation may work from home and be just a phone call away. The designer can pitch in and work on the game if the developer needs help. Video game freelancers may offer expertise in areas such as character animation, sound design, or script writing.

GAME DESIGN DOCUMENTS

Another important preproduction step is writing a detailed plan of the game. This plan is called a game design document (GDD). It describes the game for those who are building it. It outlines all the important features, including the game's story, characters, gameplay, and levels. The development team uses the GDD as a guideline for how the game should look and feel. It ensures that everyone involved in development is working toward the same goal.

FRANCHISE GAMES

Many large game publishers prefer franchise games because they are more likely to sell. These publishers need large revenue streams to keep their doors open, so they often avoid experimental games or games intended for a niche audience. Sports games such as *Madden NFL* are very popular and reliably receive a new release each year to feature the latest player rosters. Other game franchises include *Call of Duty, The Legend of Zelda,* and *Tomb Raider*. The goal of game franchises is to build a large, loyal audience. But publishers may also try out a new story or gameplay approach to attract the attention of gaming critics. Good reviews for a unique new release can lead to healthy sales.

During preproduction, concept artists may create mood boards or sketches of game elements such as characters. This artwork helps the development team figure out the right look for the game.

The GDD provides details about the rules of the game, the look of its characters, and its level of difficulty. It also includes a game pipeline, which is a timeline and list of deadlines the developer needs to meet. The game pipeline details who will be responsible for each segment of the development process. A developer must also consider any payments that will be received when it meets certain deadlines. A missed deadline could mean a delayed payment. If that happens, the whole project might shut down.

Concept artists may also contribute at this stage. They make illustrations of the game's levels, objects, and characters. The concept art gives everyone working on the game a good idea of how the finished product should look. Some concept artists use pencil drawings or paints. Others use software such as Adobe Illustrator to create digital illustrations. Artists consider the player's view of the action when drawing. This knowledge helps developers decide how a game will visually lead players through its action and levels.

PROTOTYPING

Once the GDD is completed, the game studio creates prototypes. These are early playable samples of the game. An early prototype may show off the basic way that players move through the game's environments. Later prototypes may test new ideas, scenes, or characters. If anything in the prototype feels wrong or awkward, the team makes adjustments.

Some games don't make it past the prototype stage. This might happen if a game's story isn't making sense or a game just isn't fun to play. A game that looks good on paper may not work when translated into a playable version.

At the prototype stage, developers also look for any technical issues that will affect gameplay. A specific function of a game may not work smoothly. For example, the arc of a baseball in a sports game may look wrong. Some scenes may load slowly, while others may freeze or crash. It's best to catch these technical issues at the prototype stage.

THE CERNY METHOD

Atari hired game developer Mark Cerny when he was just 17 years old. He later played a role in the creation of *Spyro the Dragon* and *Crash Bandicoot*, two of the most successful games on the original PlayStation. Along the way, Cerny learned that mistakes in preproduction were causing problems for game developers. He came up with a new way to work through this stage. He called it Method. It allows preproduction to be free of rules and structures. This provides space for new ideas as they come up. The ultimate goal is to create a "first playable," a highly polished playable portion of a game that reflects the developer's vision. The playable is used to decide whether to continue with production.

This way, the developer can fix them before moving on to the production phase, which saves time and money.

MARKETING AND MONETIZING

Another important preproduction step is determining how a game will make money. This is known as monetizing a game. The monetizing options that a developer chooses will affect the game design.

The traditional way of selling a game is to charge a single price up front, whether the game is sold in a physical retail store or as a digital download. These prices vary widely for different kinds of games. A mobile game may cost a few dollars. A blockbuster game for the latest consoles may cost $70.[3] Developers also consider whether players will be able to buy more content for the game after their initial purchase. Some games offer downloadable content (DLC), or paid expansions to a game. DLC may feature new areas to explore, new quests to complete, or new characters to play.

***Fortnite* players can purchase V-Bucks gift cards at retail stores. They use a code on the back of the card to access the virtual currency on their *Fortnite* account.**

Other games take a free-to-play approach. They can be downloaded and played at no cost, but players can purchase in-game characters and items using real money. *Fortnite*, for example, was developed by Epic Games as a free-to-play battle royale game. Players parachute onto an island where they collect weapons, build shelters, and battle other gamers until only a single player is left standing. They can use real money to purchase V-Bucks, which can be used to buy characters, costumes, and more. When a game reaches millions of players, the free-to-play strategy can be a big moneymaker. By the end of 2022, Epic had earned about $27 billion from *Fortnite*.[4]

PRODUCING PROFESSIONAL GAMES

After preproduction, a video game moves to production. During this stage, writers draft the game's story and dialogue, and programmers begin coding its gameplay. Designers are responsible for the game's characters, backgrounds, and environments. They build and refine models that are animated to walk, run, jump, and move naturally within the game. Anything the game prototype calls for, such as combat moves, weapons, and armor, is designed and tested.

Programmers must consider how game characters will interact, cooperate, or fight. They must think about how players will beat game levels. They decide what the buttons on the controller will do and how different weapons and items will function. Programmers create the systems needed for maneuvering characters and moving through environments.

When beginning a game's production phase, developers often hire a team of programmers. They seek people who have lots of experience with

Professional game studios often hire animation directors to oversee the animation production process. Mark Grigsby served as animation director for the developer Infinity Ward, working on *Call of Duty: Modern Warfare*.

game development. Many programmers have college degrees in computer science, programming, or math. They've mastered programming languages such as C++. Most have a specialty, such as graphics, animation, artificial intelligence (AI), or user interface (UI).

By this stage, the developer has chosen a game engine. Few games are programmed from scratch. Most rely on a game engine with a library of standard code that's already been written. The game engine assembles the basic elements of the game that run in the background. It may also include simple game mechanics such as running or shooting. Game engines help developers avoid a lot of repetitive coding.

TOO MANY IDEAS

The development process involves a constant flow of new ideas. Sometimes a team comes up with more ideas than will fit in a single game. While creating 2017's *The Legend of Zelda: Breath of the Wild*, the developers at Nintendo wanted to allow players to explore underground areas of the huge open-world map. But this was not feasible with the technology of the time. The team saved the idea for the 2023 sequel, *The Legend of Zelda: Tears of the Kingdom*, in which players can go underground and up to floating islands in the sky.

A MILLION DETAILS

Video games can take months or even years to produce. They may include millions of lines of programming code. For example, it took about 36 million lines of code to create the video game *Grand Theft Auto V.*[1] People were hired at different stages of the game's production process. They were assigned specific tasks. It took more than 1,000 developers three years to complete the game.[2]

MOUNIR RADI

Game directors must know about many aspects of a game, including its art, story, and mechanics. For four years, Mounir Radi filled this role for Ubisoft's game *Prince of Persia: The Lost Crown.* His work on the project began in June 2020 and continued as the game neared its release in January 2024.

Based in Montpellier, France, Radi has directed or designed several major projects. They include *ZombiU*, *Valiant Hearts: The Great War*, and *Beyond Good and Evil 2*. Radi works on concepting and prototyping games. As a game enters full production, he makes sure the team carries out the original vision.

Prince of Persia is a long-running adventure series dating back to 1989. For *The Lost Crown*, Radi wanted the game to have a fresh look and feel. Ubisoft kept *Prince of Persia*'s Middle Eastern influence in its environmental design. But Radi and his team added a flashy, anime-like art style to the game's combat scenes. He was inspired by classic fighting games.

Other *Prince of Persia* games have been 3D adventures, but Radi made *The Lost Crown* a 2D side-scroller to remind players of the very first *Prince of Persia.* He added puzzles to make the game challenging. Sargon, the game's hero, can slow down time and teleport. The game's design team also added sound effects from the original *Prince of Persia* as hidden treats for longtime fans.

Ubisoft's 2010 game *Prince of Persia: The Forgotten Sands* was popular with players. To keep up with competition in the gaming world, Radi worked to make the latest installment in the franchise unique.

MIZUNO

For a big-budget game, the production stage involves a lot of work. *Red Dead Redemption 2*, produced by Rockstar Games, contains 300,000 animations and 500,000 lines of dialogue.[3] Each animation must be designed and programmed, and each line of dialogue must be written and recorded.

Cinematic scenes, also known as cutscenes, must also be planned and animated during this stage. This is slow, painstaking work. During preproduction, a previsualization animator works on camera angles and character placement. Every detail is mapped out and carefully timed. Animators may complete just a few seconds of a cutscene in one workday. Because this work takes so much time, many developers hire outside studios to complete cutscenes.

MOTION CAPTURE AND ART

Motion capture technology, also known as mocap, has become a key element in video game production. This process usually takes place in a studio. Actors wear body suits covered in sensors. A camera follows the actors as they perform game actions such as jumping, rolling, or climbing. Computer systems capture the motion and store it as data files. Programmers then incorporate these files into game scenes, using the actors' movements to animate game characters. Mocap helps developers create more realistic character animations for games.

Motion capture makes it easier for developers to animate complex character movements. This technology can also capture actors' facial expressions, allowing developers to make photorealistic characters.

THE LIBRARY

An important part of video game production is building the developer's library, or collection of game assets. This refers to the digital files that make up the game's visual and audio content, including 3D models, textures, songs, and sound effects. A developer's library grows with each new game it makes. An object from an old game might be stored in the library. Programmers can pull that object from the library, edit it, and insert it into the code for a new game. A well-organized library saves developers time when creating a new game.

Art directors oversee the designers who create a game's visuals, including character models, backgrounds, animations, or special effects. Dozens of artists may contribute to a game. They may use design software such as Adobe Photoshop, Adobe After Effects, or Adobe Premiere Pro. Their work must be scheduled in a logical sequence. A character can't be designed firing a weapon, for example, until the weapon has been designed. The developer uses a pipeline document to keep the teams on schedule.

PROGRAMMING

Programmers have specific roles during production. Physics programmers create the movement of a game's characters and objects. They might be tasked with creating something unique for a game. This might be the illusion of bounding down the walls of skyscrapers in a *Spider-Man* game. Or it might be the parachute drop that begins each match in *Fortnite*. Video games are all about visual excitement, so developers aim to create visuals that will capture players' attention.

AI programmers are responsible for how a video game reacts to a player's actions. They may program a game so that as it continues, enemies get smarter and can predict a

Some professional game companies employ thousands of people and have multiple branches. Ubisoft, for example, has more than 45 studios in 30 countries around the world.

MASERATI
iiyama

Professional game studios hire sound designers to record, edit, and mix sound effects for a game. Sound designers must make sure sound effects match the game's tone and work well with the gameplay.

player's next move. Input programmers work on the game inputs and outputs. An input is an action performed by the player, such as clicking the left mouse button or tilting the thumb sticks on a controller. Input programmers must consider how inputs translate to actions on the screen and how the game reacts. UI programmers create screens and menus that offer information to the player. These features might include the startup screen, settings menu, or scoreboard. Network programmers handle the functions needed for online gaming. Sound programmers integrate voices, music, and sound effects into the game.

MEETING MILESTONES

During production, game development teams must meet certain milestones, or goals. These are determined and agreed upon by the publisher and developer. The publisher releases a payment for the next stage once the previous milestone is reached. This allows the developer to pay the team members. It's also an incentive to move the game production process forward as efficiently as possible.

If problems arise during production, the process may slow down. The game may stretch the limits of the hardware. A battle sequence may not work properly. A level may be slow to load. A twist in a game's story might not make sense. When these issues come up, the design team is called in to make any necessary changes.

One key milestone is the alpha version of the game. A complete alpha release includes all key functions, gameplay, and levels. It also includes the game's completed artwork, dialogue, and sound. No major additions to the game take place after the alpha stage. The only changes allowed after this point are adjustments to solve glitches and smooth rough edges.

At late stages in the development process, teams may face what is known as crunch. This industry term refers to the practice of teams working many extra hours to finish a game and get it ready for release by a certain date. During crunch, workers may have very little downtime. They often deal with fatigue, exhaustion, and burnout. The stress has driven many dedicated video game creators out of the business. Reporting by game journalists has brought more attention to this issue. Some companies are working to end the practice to promote a healthier work-life balance for their teams.

TESTING THE GAME

Next, a video game reaches the beta stage. At this point, the game goes through a lot of testing. Testers from outside the company are brought in to play every part of the game and identify any problems that need fixing. Testers also focus on playability and fun. They must consider several big questions. Is the game entertaining and interesting? Does the story make sense? Is the ending satisfying? Is the game worth the money and time required to play it?

> **"In the end, what you're responsible for as a game designer is whether a game is fun or not.[4]"**
>
> ***—Paolo Malabuyo, former lead game designer at Microsoft***

Outside beta testers might see things in the game that the in-house teams missed. Under the pressure of deadlines, programmers and artists can easily overlook things. Beta testers may also catch more serious problems, such as a bug that might freeze the game or crash the console. Releasing the game without resolving these issues could be a disaster. The reputation of the publisher and developer is on the line.

Following the beta stage, a game goes through its final testing. After this, a game is said to have gone gold. This means the game is finally ready for release. It is sent to a game disc or cartridge manufacturer or uploaded to digital stores.

In the meantime, the publisher prepares for the game's release. The publisher buys advertising and promotes the game through the media. It collects preorders from eager customers. The publisher also negotiates with retailers, deciding how many copies of the game stores will need from the initial shipment.

Nobody can know for sure what kind of demand a game will have after it is released. Making video games is a business, but it's also an art form. How the public will respond to a game is a mystery until sales numbers start coming in.

BETA TESTERS

It may sound like beta testers get paid to play video games. But this is not as fun as it might seem. Testers replay small sections of games assigned by the developer. They test every possible action and character over and over again to look for bugs. This can involve many hours of replaying a single game scene. Beta testers are usually not paid much and have little room for career advancement if they don't have experience with design or programming. It's a hard job, so many eager newcomers drop out of it quickly.

GameStop
106
SALE
We Buy Your Electronics & Games for Cash or Credit
oculus
SALE
Holiday
DEALS

POSTPRODUCTION FOR PROFESSIONAL GAMES

The video game market is very competitive. Dozens of major games are released each year, along with thousands of smaller ones. All of them compete for attention and money. They also compete with movie theaters, streaming services, music, and other forms of entertainment.

The production of a new video game can take years and cost a publisher millions of dollars. Because of this huge investment, a publisher's primary goal is to release the game on schedule with as few bugs as possible. But even when the game is ready to ship, the work isn't done. The publisher still needs to make the game stand out. This postproduction stage is about marketing a game, supporting it after launch, and fixing any remaining bugs.

REVIEWS AND ADVERTISING

By the time a game comes out, the publisher has often already sent early versions of the game to reviewers. This ensures that people can post game reviews online

In 2022, video game sales in the United States brought in billions of dollars. Many games are sold at stores such as GameStop, the largest video game retailer in the world.

Gaming publications such as *PC Gamer* can be good marketing and research tools for developers. These outlets often include reviews and news about upcoming games.

before launch day. If the reviews are positive, they can help generate excitement for the game and increase sales. Publishers also run advertisements on game sites and social media. Quotes from positive reviews often appear in these ads.

Game publishers can use several tools to promote their products. In the past, game companies placed advertisements in traditional print media, such as magazines. Long-running magazines such as *Nintendo Power* and *Electronic Gaming Monthly* were popular in the 1990s and early 2000s. Companies with bigger budgets could afford television ads. They also sent press releases to the media to raise awareness of new games.

Today, game publishers focus more of their efforts on promoting new releases online. They run advertisements on gaming websites. Publishers such as Sony, Microsoft, and Nintendo operate websites and social media channels, as do game developers of all sizes. Individual games may even have their own Facebook and Instagram profiles. When fans stream gameplay on Twitch or post videos of themselves playing a game on YouTube, this content can serve as free advertising too.

CYBERPUNK 2077

If a game is not properly debugged, it can fail in the market. In late 2020, the developer CD Projekt Red released *Cyberpunk 2077*. The hotly anticipated open-world RPG was full of bugs and other issues. Sony even pulled it from the PlayStation store. But CD Projekt Red worked to fix the game. Nearly three years later, it released version 2.0 of the game. The company not only cleaned up the bugs but also rethought significant parts of the game's design. Many critics praised the update, with Tom Senior of Eurogamer writing, "It's rare to see a game reworked so thoroughly, and rarer still to see such an update succeed quite so well."[1]

VIDEO GAME TRAILERS

Video game trailers are key marketing tools for game publishers. These videos can make upcoming games look exciting and interesting to players. But sometimes, video game trailers can mislead players. Some game publishers have put out prerelease trailers that deliberately avoid spoiling major plot points. The popular character Joel from *The Last of Us* seemed to be prominently featured in the trailer for the game's sequel, *The Last of Us Part II*. But in the final game, Joel actually dies early in the story. Many fans had been looking forward to playing as Joel and felt cheated by the trailer.

Mobile game publishers work to make their games as visible as possible. This means making sure a game appears in search results when people search on app stores. The publisher will carefully select keywords and screenshots, write exciting game descriptions, and upload video trailers. This can increase the chances of potential buyers checking out the game.

GAME UPDATES

Although the developer may have thoroughly tested the game, it may still have problems. After a game's release, developers continue to support it with updates. Feedback from players influences these adjustments and fixes.

During this time, publishers pay attention to social media and video game fan sites. Their marketing teams also read media reviews, such as those in the magazines *PC Gamer* and *Game Informer*. Platforms such as Steam offer player reviews and comments too. On Steam, gamers can post their own screenshots of games and rack up achievements as they progress or find hidden treasures in a game.

When games were released on CDs, adding content or fixing bugs after release was impossible. The game had to be fully completed upon release. But in the age of internet-connected consoles, postlaunch updates are common.

CONVENTIONS

Game publishers may participate in gaming conventions. Popular gaming conventions include the Tokyo Game Show and Penny Arcade Expo (PAX), which is held in various cities each year. Big conventions also take place in Brazil, the United Kingdom, and Germany. Some major game publishers operate their own events.

Conventions can be a great way for companies to advertise new games. But they require time, money, and planning. Publishers must rent booth space, prepare flyers and merchandise, and set up demo stations where attendees can sample playable levels of upcoming games. They may have writers, designers, and other employees mingle with the attendees or hold panel discussions. They may even hire people to dress up as characters from their games.

Games that are a hit at a big convention can gain the attention of the media. Word of mouth is valuable in any entertainment business. To generate buzz for their games, many publishers will promote games that are still in development or at the concept stage. They can tease these upcoming releases with short video trailers.

People who attend gaming conventions are often looking for something to talk about. Game publishers try to provide that. That's why publishers strive to develop impressive new gameplay or equipment that players haven't encountered before.

INFLUENCERS

Social media influencers offer another way for game publishers to market their releases. Influencers are social media stars who promote various products to their online audiences. This may include video games and gaming equipment. By posting videos about their gaming experience, influencers can broaden a game's audience. They may post on sites such as YouTube, Instagram, or Twitch.

The company Supercell created the mobile game *Brawl Stars*. It partnered with ten influencers to promote the game before its release, focusing on people who were already creating content based on the company's other games. The influencers ran live gameplay streams to show

Gaming conventions are held in large spaces and have thousands of attendees. At these events, developers can market their games by setting up display booths and gaming stations.

STARS OF THE GAMES

Some developers hire Hollywood stars to play important roles in their video games, potentially drawing more attention to the project. *Alone in the Dark* is a reboot of a long-running series of survival horror games. In the game, published by THQ Nordic, players can select one of two characters to play. They can be Emily Hartwood, the niece of the victim, or Edward Carnby, a private detective. Hartwood is played by actress Jodie Comer from the hit TV show *Killing Eve*. Carnby is played by David Harbour, who played Chief Jim Hopper in the Netflix show *Stranger Things*.

off *Brawl Stars*. The game saw five million registrations after the release date was announced, in part due to Supercell's innovative marketing strategy.[2]

POSTLAUNCH CONTENT

In the 2010s, DLC became a popular way for publishers to earn more money from a game after its initial release. DLC may include new game levels, characters, or chapters of a game. DLC allows a publisher to keep a game fresh and interesting for the players who most enjoy playing it. It gives the game replay value, making players want to return to the game even after completing it to check out the new content.

Some game publishers have also made multiplayer online games part of their postlaunch marketing. Live-service games, such as *Destiny 2* and *Fortnite*, feature a steady stream of new content. Some content is free to all players, while some requires paying a fee. Live events, such as tournaments, can bring together massive audiences at a certain date or time. Large development teams are needed to support this ongoing work. With live-service games, the development process never truly ends.

The creators of *Brawl Stars* made special game characters for each of the influencers it partnered with. This helped get the influencers' followers interested in the game, increasing engagement.

Some game developers announce DLC or game updates at events such as conferences.

THE POSTMORTEM

In the meantime, a game's production team usually holds a postmortem meeting. During this meeting, they discuss the game's development and identify things that went wrong. This helps the team improve the development process for future projects. Team members may also talk about how the project's planning and scheduling could have been improved.

A postmortem document provides the entire story of a game's creation, from concept to release. It may make suggestions about how to streamline or improve the production process for future games. It may also list team members who came up with good solutions or went above and beyond in their work.

During postproduction, the developer also prepares a closing kit, or archive. This is a collection of game assets, including design documents, programming code, character models, and music files. It sets down the entire production process as a permanent record. The assets go into a library, and developers can borrow them for future games. A closing kit is useful if developers need a game's original assets for upgrades, DLC, or sequels. If a game sells well, it may be ported to a new platform or issued in different languages for foreign markets.

> **"It's about understanding your audience and tailoring content to be relevant. That's where micro and mid-tier influencers come in. They often have more dedicated audiences, which brands can tap into.[3]"**
>
> ***—Robin Åström, CEO of a video game marketing agency, 2022***

EGGS
IS FUEL
WORLDS ADRIFT

MAKING INDIE VIDEO GAMES

Many types of video games are available, from casual mobile games to complicated RPGs. If people stick to one kind of game, they may have ideas about how to improve the genre. Some even try making their own games. The trend in games developed by soloists or small companies has inspired a new wave of independent, or indie, game production.

Indie games are made by small companies or individuals working outside the commercial mainstream. They are the opposite of big-budget franchise games. The cost of making an indie game is much lower, and fewer people are involved in making it. The process of creating indie games is usually less complicated too.

Smaller game developers can take more risks than big-budget developers. It's easier for them to change course in the middle of a project. To improve a game, they might rewrite its story. They might come up with different characters or bosses. If a larger game developer wanted to do this, it would likely have to create a library of new assets and delay the game's release.

London-based indie developer Bossa Games took off when it made *Surgeon Simulator*. The company has participated in game jams, events in which teams brainstorm and create a video game from scratch in a limited time.

THE FIRST INDIE BLOCKBUSTER

While working at the Russian Academy of Sciences in the 1980s, Alexey Pajitnov designed the game *Tetris*. In this 2D puzzle game, a series of different shapes made from four squares drop from the top of the screen. Players try to change and move the shapes so they form a complete row when they reach the bottom. This engaging gameplay quickly hooked players. After Pajitnov created the game, he partnered with game publisher Henk Rogers. The pair licensed the game to Nintendo. Since then, *Tetris* has spread to more than 50 different platforms.[1] It's considered the most successful indie game ever made.

GOING SOLO

In part, the indie wave has been a pushback against the massive growth of the video game industry. Many gamers don't like the predictable franchise games produced by large publishers. They're searching for games with the creativity and individuality that made early games so memorable.

In some ways, it's easier for individuals to create a game. In the past, game creators had to master programming code. But now, specialized software allows individuals to make video games without having to do much coding. People can use online software tools, character models, and gameplay templates. Beginners can use open-source software, which comes with prewritten code that developers can access, edit, and customize to create games. Some tools, such as Godot Engine and Twine, are free. Others, such as RPG Maker and GameMaker, cost money.

As game development tools become more accessible and easy to use, the field of independent game development is getting bigger. The competition is getting keener too. It's tough to make a game stand out in a crowded field. In order to make a profitable game, indie developers search for a niche.

People interested in making indie games can get started by learning how to use game engines and design tools.

Color Properties

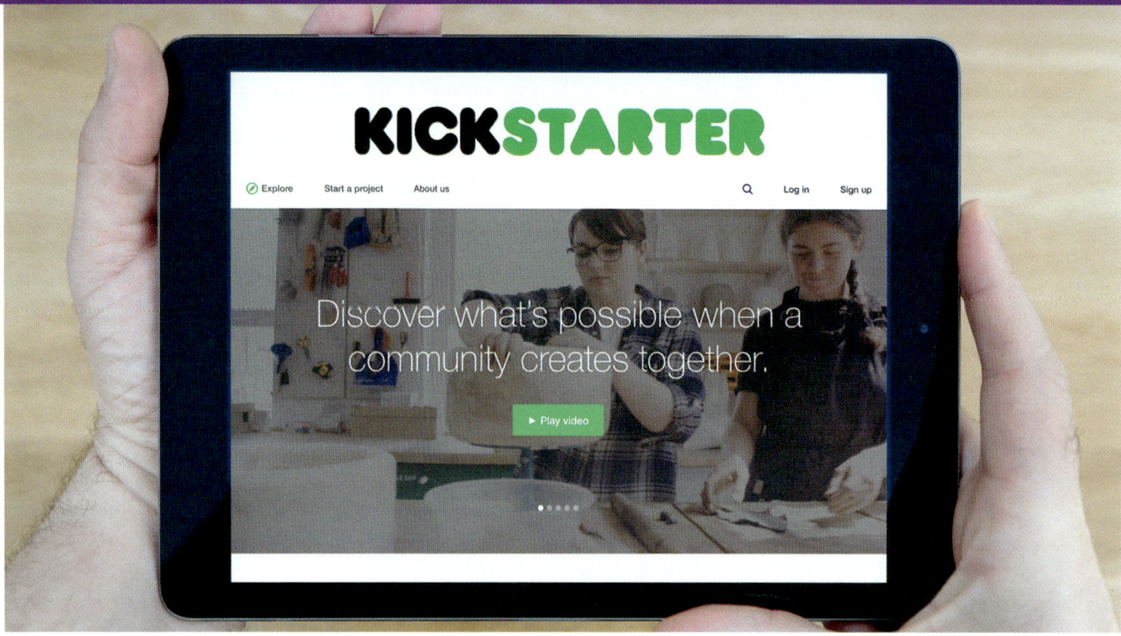

Through its Kickstarter campaign, indie developer Heart Machine was able to raise more than $645,000 for the game *Hyper Light Drifter*.

This can be something in the gameplay, story, art style, or characters that makes their brand distinct.

FIRST STEPS

All video games require investment. For AAA games, a publisher provides money so the developer can keep the production process going. But indie developers must raise money on their own before or during the production process. They do this by creating a business plan and budget. The budget is an estimate of the total cost of the game's development. The developer's plan may also propose ways to secure money from investors.

Investors may be individuals, game studios, or publishers. The game's creators can also invest their own money. Investors often want to see a plan and know all about a game. Indie developers must provide a schedule for the game's release and information about the game's intended audience.

Crowdsourcing is a key source of financial support for many indie developers. It involves raising small donations from large numbers of people through a website such as GoFundMe, Patreon, or Kickstarter. The developer announces and describes their game, gives a release date, sets a goal for contributions, and provides updates on the game's progress. They may release short trailers or provide discounted games for supporters.

The developer Heart Machine used Kickstarter to raise funds for the game *Hyper Light Drifter*. The Heart Machine team provided demos of the game and stayed in touch with its Kickstarter contributors. Drawing on players' comments, the team tweaked the game during production. They used several types of software and graphic design tools, including GameMaker, Adobe Photoshop, and Adobe After Effects. The improved version of *Hyper Light Drifter* offered less exploration and more combat. The game was a success when it was released in 2015. Heart Machine

USERS PITCH IN

Many indie developers like to keep their players involved. This means doing more than just selling them games. Many indie developers accept user-generated content (UGC) in their games. They allow players to upload new characters, tools, or art to the game. Game engines such as Unity make this easy to do. The software provides a content creation tool and a "bridge" so that new content can be sent to the developer. After making sure the UGC meets the game's guidelines, the developer offers it to all players to try out and review.

went on to produce the games *Hyper Light Breaker* and *Solar Ash*.

Funding can also come out of the creator's own pocket or from their families. At age 12, Xalavier Nelson Jr. discovered that game publishers would send free games to reviewers. As a teen, Nelson worked as a freelance writer for *PC Gamer* and other magazines. Although he dreamed of making his own games, Nelson had learned about tough conditions and long workdays in game studios. So he decided to strike out on his own and try indie development.

Nelson found joy and satisfaction in making video games. His early credits include *An Airport for Aliens Currently Run by Dogs* and *Space Warlord Organ Trading Simulator*. In 2019, with $2,000 in start-up money donated by his father, Nelson founded the indie studio Strange Scaffold.[2] By 2023, the studio had released seven games, including *El Paso, Elsewhere*. The studio uses Unity to create its games. For his creative work, Nelson was nominated for a British Academy of Film and TV (BAFTA) video game award.

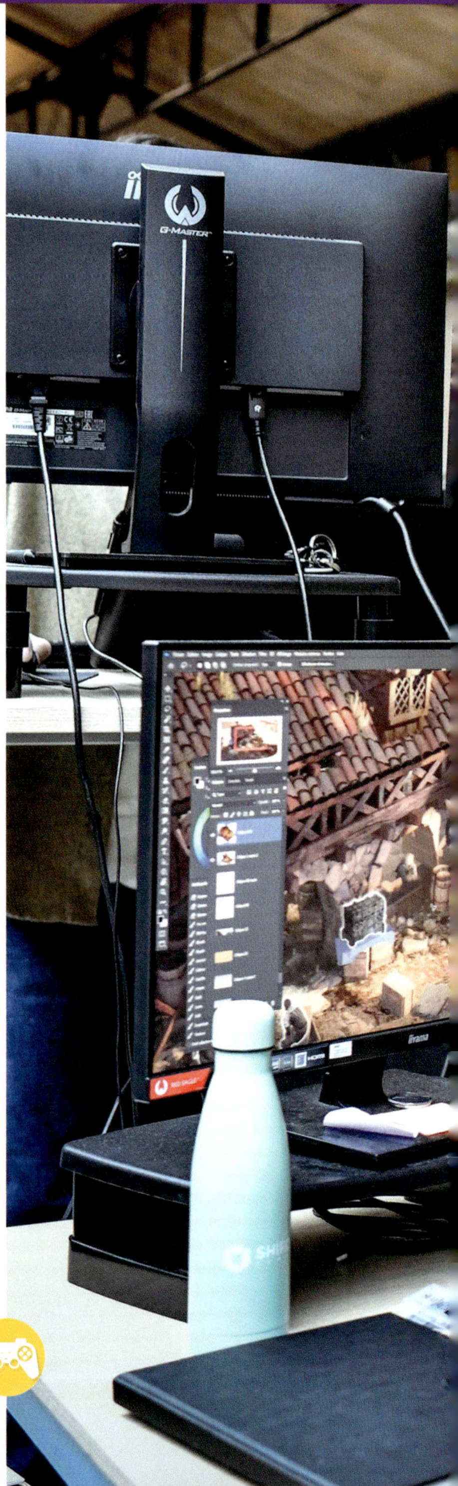

Indie development teams often spend time making a distinct brand and style for their games. Many fans like indie games because they have unique stories and eye-catching designs.

iiyama

BUILDING TEAMS

New game developers quickly learn that game production has many facets. A single developer may be an expert in an important skill, such as designing 3D environments. But they may have little experience in writing dialogue, creating music, or marketing games. They need colleagues who can provide these skills.

Many developers who work for indie game companies already have experience. They may have started out as employees with big production companies but eventually sought more creative freedom. Brendon Chung, for example, left Pandemic Studios after Electronic Arts bought the company. He founded Blendo Games, working with a small team to make games such as *Atom Zombie Smasher* and *Flotilla*. Blendo's game *Quadrilateral Cowboy* won the 2017 Independent Games Festival prize for best independent game.

> **"Burnout is so endemic in this industry because every single project carries the potential consequence of your career being over.[3]"**
>
> ***—Xalavier Nelson Jr. on tough working conditions in the game industry***

Like professional game developers, indie developers may hire a variety of team members and specialists to work on a game. They may hire artists to develop the game's look and feel. An important ingredient for a successful indie developer is to have an eye-catching style that helps build an identifiable brand. Heart Machine's games, for example, are known for their open worlds and elaborate fantasy artwork. Indie developers must also pick a software to use. Unity and Unreal Engine are two of the most popular engines among indie developers.

> **You can make an amazing game, but you can't make a success. Your players make the success.**[4]
>
> ***—Imre Jele, cofounder of Bossa Games***

Indie developers also may need writers, programmers, and sound designers. If their game requires a story and dialogue, they'll need to hire writers. Programmers can fill multiple roles. They may build the game using programming code, handle testing and debugging, and create menus. Other staff members may also have multiple roles to play. A character designer may be asked to design a new level map or UI. A voice actor who does musical performances may pitch in with the game's sound effects and background music.

As they grow, indie developers may create more specialized roles for employees. If the company has grown and has several games in its pipeline, it will need project managers. These managers may cover multiple roles, such as overseeing the art team, hiring freelancers, and updating schedules. A project manager lays down the milestones that the game needs to meet and coordinates the work of different teams to make sure the process moves forward at a good pace.

After creating a game prototype as a student, Nina Freeman led a small team as project manager. "It was super hard," she said. "I learned a lot about how important it is to check in with teammates regularly to make sure everyone was on the same page. . . . It's easy to get lost in one feature or part of the game, but it's more important to keep pushing forward, even if every little thing you make isn't perfect."[5]

PLAYING IN THE SANDBOX

In 2009, 30-year-old computer programmer Markus Persson was living in Stockholm, Sweden. When he wasn't working, he was at home coding video games. When Persson's latest creation was ready, he posted it to an online gaming forum. It was a sandbox game that allowed players to design and build things. He coded it using the Lightweight Java Game Library, an open-source software tool. Persson was a big fan of Lego blocks, so he chose square-shaped building blocks as the game's central element. He called the game *Minecraft*.

Over the next few months, *Minecraft* attracted many new players. In 2010, Persson decided to quit his job, start a company, and keep developing the game. By the next year, the game had millions of fans. After five more years of tweaking and improving *Minecraft*, Persson sold his company to Microsoft for $2.5 billion.[6]

Some indie game developers are inspired by existing franchises. They might believe they have a better way to make a popular game. Others create new spins on games they enjoy. Eric Barone loved to play *Harvest Moon*. In this game, players became

***Minecraft* continues to be a popular game for both younger and older audiences. By October 2023, more than 300 million copies of the game had been sold worldwide.**

Crafting
Inventory
XDK

Within just two months of *Stardew Valley*'s 2016 release, more than one million copies of the game had been sold. In March 2022, that number had grown to more than 20 million.

virtual farmers. Barone admired the simple gameplay and peaceful atmosphere of *Harvest Moon* but thought he could do better. So he started programming in his spare time. During a four-year period, Barone created characters, scenery, and music.

He wrote the game's code using Microsoft XNA Game Studio software and the MonoGame engine. He spent many hours making the game while working part time as a theater usher. When the game was ready, Barone released it as *Stardew Valley*.

Barone's game was a massive hit. People of all ages enjoyed it, even those who had no experience playing video games. Many *Stardew Valley* fans see the game as an escape from typical gameplay, along with the stresses of modern life and work.

Barone and Persson created successful video games completely on their own. They worked as independent game developers with no game publisher backing them. But this is a rare achievement in the video game industry. Most indie games are created by following the usual game production processes. But with smaller budgets, the people who make these games work at a smaller scale.

THE *SPELUNKY* STORY

Designing a video game and running a game studio involves many steps. This process can sometimes bring frustration and disappointment. But indie game developer Derek Yu handled this on his own. Yu was a computer science student in California when he created *Spelunky*. In this retro-style platformer game, players venture underground to fight monsters, collect treasure, and escape traps. *Spelunky* became one of the most popular indie games of the 2010s. Encouraged by the game's success, Yu founded the game studio Mossmouth. He also has a personal website that provides game development tutorials and guides.

CHAPTER **SEVEN**

MARKETING INDIE GAMES

Once an indie game is complete, the creator must sell it. That means letting the public and any potential buyers know about the game. Reviews, advertising, and promotion are necessary parts of this process. Because marketing video games is an important aspect of making them, many big companies prepare large marketing budgets. Bungie Software spent $80 million to market *Halo 2,* and Rockstar Games budgeted $200 million to promote *Red Dead Redemption 2*.[1]

Indie developers have smaller budgets than professional game developers, but they must still spend money on marketing. The amount of money for marketing is typically proportional to a game's development budget. This percentage varies but usually falls within the range of twenty-five to fifty cents for every dollar spent on creating the game.[2]

Marketing indie games is different from marketing professional ones. AAA games target a large, market-tested, easily identifiable gaming audience.

Partnering with influencers or gaming streamers can be a good way for indie developers to market their games and expand their audiences.

MOBILE GAMES

More than 1.5 billion people worldwide play mobile games, such as those on smartphones.[3] These popular games provide entertainment for all ages. Many first-time game designers choose to create mobile games. Compared with consoles and PCs, mobile phones are an easy platform for new programmers. But mobile games also go through trends, and what sells well in the market changes. Mobile game developers aim to catch the latest trendy wave with perfect timing and a good game.

Before building the game, they figure out whether it will sell and which gamers will enjoy it. Indie game developers are usually less interested in market testing or catering to a wide audience. This gives them greater creative freedom when making their games, along with fewer marketing expenses.

Many indie developers target niche markets. These are small subsets, such as the age range, education level, or location of the target audience. For example, a cheerleader murder mystery game may be targeted at teenage girls. A puzzle game modeled after Scrabble may be aimed at middle-aged players.

Unlike professional game developers, indie developers don't have to worry about publishers or clients pushing them to meet a release date. But having a release date for an indie game is still crucial. Promising a release by a certain date keeps potential players interested.

One marketing tactic for indie developers is a soft launch. This involves releasing a game to a small, restricted audience, such as the people who donated to the developer through crowdfunding. The developer seeks feedback from the group. Are there any bugs and crashes? Do the controls work smoothly? What's fun about the game? The developer can then tweak the game if necessary, improving it for the official public launch.

LEE HUTCHINSON

As a kid, Lee Hutchinson was obsessed with computer games. After beating a game, he would keep playing it over and over. Finally, the only thing left to do was study the computer's programming manual. In this way, Hutchinson taught himself computer programming.

After graduating from Teesside University in Middlesbrough, England, Hutchinson held programming and management roles at Venom Games, Rockstar Leeds, 2K Games, and Rare. He went on to found his own game publishing studio, Double Eleven. This company licenses games from major publishers such as Sony and Microsoft. It ports the games to new platforms and mobile devices.

One of Double Eleven's most successful productions has been a console port of the popular PC game *Goat Simulator*. It sold more than one million units. After starting up in Hutchinson's home, Double Eleven now has 300 employees. Hutchinson is the company's CEO. The company has studios in the United Kingdom and Kuala Lumpur, Malaysia.[4]

Double Eleven worked with developer Coffee Stain Studios on the game *Goat Simulator*. Since then, several new versions of the game have been made.

For most indie games, the launch date is the day on which the game is made available to players online. Developers using online platforms may have prepared for this day by uploading videos or demos to the game page. Few indie games are sold through retail outlets. Unlike commercial publishers, indie developers don't have agreements in place to sell through stores such as GameStop or big retailers such as Target.

Fortunately, indie developers are less dependent on big sales numbers than professional developers. Profit margins are better online than they are through retail outlets. What indie developers seek is a loyal audience—gamers who look forward to their next game. The downside is that their games are made on small budgets. This means indie developers may be unable to withstand projects that fail in the market or get suspended during production.

> **"If your players have certain expectations, you need to meet them. . . . And if you're good at what you do, you will know your players' expectations.[5]"**
>
> ***—Nika Bender, game producer***

FINDING A DISTRIBUTOR

Once an indie game is complete, the developer must decide how to advertise and sell it. Some independent creators partner with commercial publishers. Publishers have the resources to effectively market video games. They also have media connections. With these connections, publishers can get games reviewed in the press. This coverage can help developers build an audience for a game. But finding a publisher is not easy. Game creators must pitch their game to a publisher and prove that it will sell. The publisher may consider if there is already a market for the game. The publisher may also consider whether the developer will be able to produce the game on their own or if they have a team and budget for the project.

Most indie developers choose to go without a publisher. This gives the developer control over how their game looks and works. They set their own timetable and release date. They make all the marketing decisions. There's also no need to share the money the game makes, although developers may need to pay royalties to a selling platform.

Indie developers who distribute their games without a publisher sell their work on platforms such as Steam, the Epic Games Store, or the App Store. When a player buys a game, these platforms take a percentage of the selling price. They pay the rest to the developer. Itch.io, a platform dedicated to indie games, allows the developer to set the royalty percentage. Developers can put their games up for sale on the platform and decide what percentage of the sale goes to itch.io.

MONETIZING WITH THE APP STORE

Game developers must consider how to monetize their games. For mobile games, this often means using Apple's App Store. Here, customers can browse, buy, and download a variety of smartphone and tablet apps. Apple takes a percentage of these sales. But by using the App Store, game developers can access a huge, eager market. In 2009, the App Store began offering in-app purchases. After downloading an app or game, players could buy new features or levels. This provided an ongoing stream of income for game developers. It also meant games could be offered for free or for lower prices in the App Store.

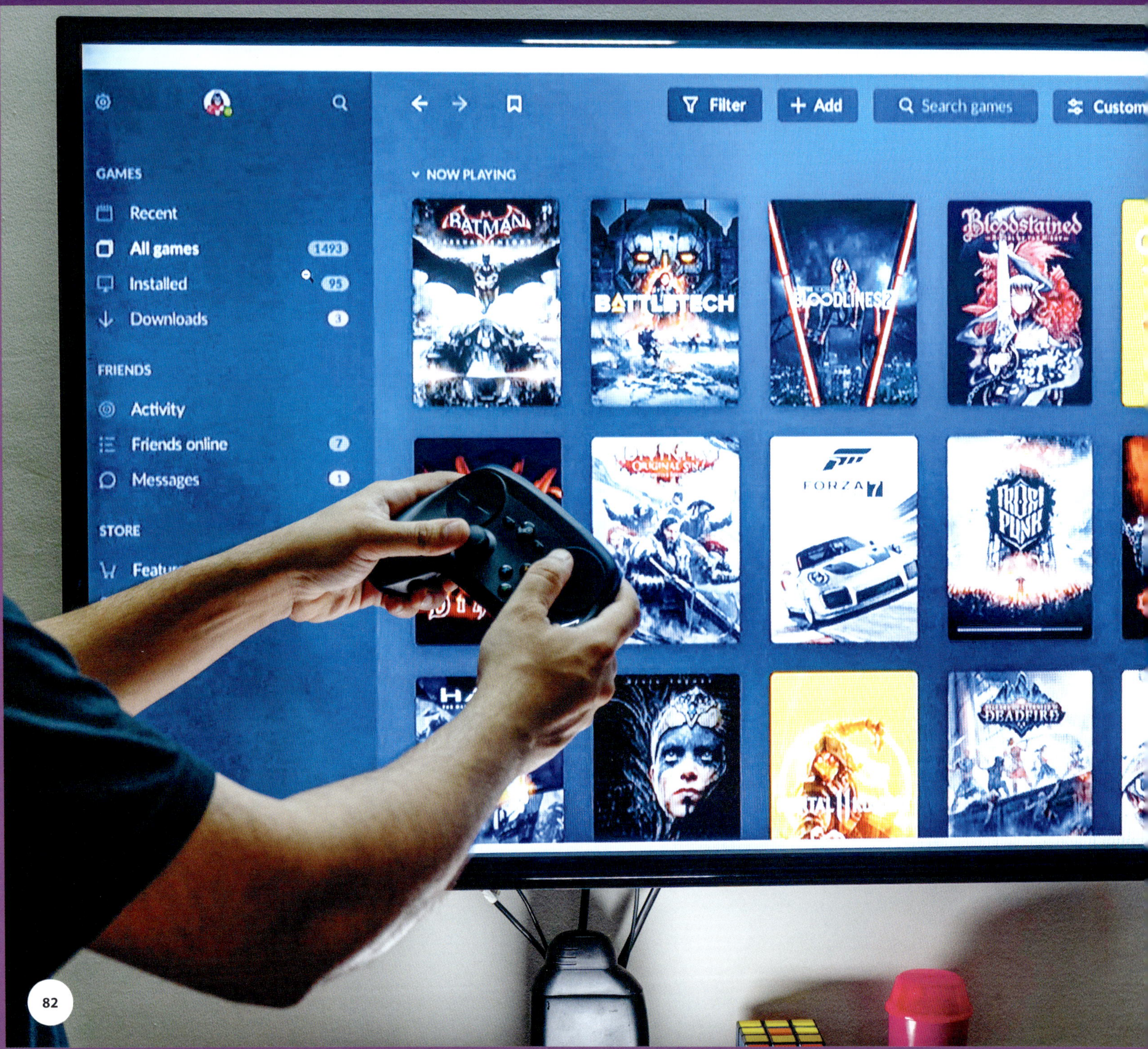

Filter
+ Add
Search games
GAMES
Recent
All games
1493
Installed
95
Downloads
3
FRIENDS
Activity
Friends online
7
Messages
1
STORE
NOW PLAYING
BATMAN
BATTLETECH
BLOODLINES 2
Bloodstained
FORZA 7
FROSTPUNK

Each platform has rules about how games can be sold on their sites. The Steam platform, for instance, offers Steam Direct. This is a way to submit and sell new games. First, developers pay a fee. Then they build a store page with screenshots and marketing text, upload the latest version of the game, and select their pricing. Steam reviews the game and makes sure it runs properly. Creating a store page before release allows the developer to build public interest in their game, answer players' questions, and take part in discussions.

Once a developer decides how to sell a game, it can raise interest by releasing trailers and demos for the game. Video game trailers often appear on YouTube, Facebook, and other video-sharing sites. A demo is a short playable version of a game. It features important game mechanics and takes the player through a sample part of the game. The Steam Next Fest is an event that offers hundreds of demos to potential buyers, bringing a big audience to indie developers three times a year.

Players who enjoy the demo of a video game will likely stay tuned for the game's release. They are also likely to buy the game when it comes out. Demos are also a good way to draw the most skilled players into the beta testing process. These people are asked to play-test the game and give feedback to the developer. In the meantime, beta testers spread the word about the upcoming game to their friends and social media acquaintances.

Steam grants gamers access to thousands of different games. Users can buy new games, chat in message boards, and live stream. The platform's popularity attracts many game developers.

CONNECTING WITH PLAYERS

Daisuke Amaya didn't have a marketing plan for *Cave Story*. But he had ideas about how to connect with gamers and develop a fan base. He made sure that news of the game spread on gaming message boards. That way, *Cave Story*'s market was already established by the time the game was ready for release. Although Amaya didn't have a publisher partner or advertising budget, *Cave Story* became an instant hit.

For indie creators, building a loyal audience for their brand is important. A big commercial publisher can depend on buyers for franchises such as *Spider-Man* or *The Legend of Zelda*. Players who enjoy these games often don't pay much attention to who publishes or develops them. But indie games don't market themselves, and without a distinctive brand to sell, small developers will remain unknown. Even if an indie developer has already released a few games, it may struggle to sell its next release in big numbers. Competition is heavy in the indie games space, where hundreds of other companies are also doing business.

> **"Maybe the individual pixels on one portrait don't matter, but the general approach of being meticulous and caring about details—that approach overall led to it being a good game.[6]"**
>
> ***—Eric Barone, on his game*** **Stardew Valley**

One solution is connection. An indie developer can engage with its audience by showing up at conventions, creating user-friendly websites, releasing free demos, and responding to feedback. Many indie developers invite gamers to be active participants in the process. They accept suggestions, respond to complaints, and tweak games according to surveys, emails, and message boards.

AGENCY MARKETING

Making connections can cost indie developers time and money. An indie developer who must concentrate on making a game may handle the marketing only part-time. Responding to messages, posting updates, and building websites may not interest the developer as much as designing, coding, or writing the game.

For this reason, indie developers with a large enough budget sometimes choose agency marketing. They hire a company that specializes in promoting and advertising products and companies. Agencies take on the developer's marketing tasks full-time. By signing a contract with an agency, a game developer can set down exactly what's expected, create an advertising budget, and agree to a timetable for a game's release.

The agency might handle publicity by offering news about the game to newspapers, magazines, and review sites such

SELLING ON THE WEB

Not all game creators use Steam, the App Store, or other online platforms to sell their games. They may want control over their marketing and hope to avoid conforming to platform standards. Many developers don't want to pay a big percentage of their earnings to a platform. Some choose to market their games through their own websites and social media profiles. Websites allow developers to present their games in more detail and communicate directly with their audiences. This can help create a base of loyal fans who will follow an indie developer as they make new content and games.

Indie developers can use social media and streaming sites such as Twitch to connect with their players. Twitch even has an online guide for game developers interested in using the platform.

as Metacritic. The agency may also have a team that creates and maintains a website or app for the game. This site may invite users to explore the game through summaries, character descriptions, screenshots, videos, and demos. The site may also allow early players to post comments about the game.

Agencies can also help with posting and selling the game. This may happen on platforms such as Steam, the App Store, and the Epic Games Store. Agencies know the costs and benefits of these platforms and help developers decide which one to use.

Sometimes agencies help plan global media tours, in which game developers travel to meetings, conventions, and tournaments to promote their game. Game marketing agencies may reach out to influencers on Twitch, a site that allows users to stream their gameplay for an audience. Agencies may post videos of upcoming games to YouTube and Instagram too. They can build Facebook pages and Twitter feeds. The goal is to get a game in front of as many people as possible, expanding its audience.

Smartphone Game Area
スマートフォン
ゲーム
コーナー
KONAMI
EA SPORTS
FC24
EA SPORTS
FC24
EA SPORTS FC
WELCOME TO THE CLUB
FC24
試遊列最後尾
出口

CHAPTER **EIGHT**

THE FUTURE OF VIDEO GAMES

Video game technology changes all the time. Because of this, game developers must pay attention to the market. People are always looking for the latest developments in the gaming world. Game publishers who can't meet players' changing expectations may struggle to find an audience.

GAMING TRENDS AND TECHNOLOGIES

Developers can learn more about gaming industry trends by reading reviews, following gaming news, and playing the latest releases themselves. But to fully understand new game technology, developers must talk with fellow game makers and gamers. One way to do this is by attending gaming conventions.

The video game industry is well suited to conventions because it is a social business. Companies and their leaders always have new things to show off and share. Developers take every chance they can to interact with the gaming public.

More than 240,000 people attended the 2023 Tokyo Game Show. The event featured more than 2,000 games and booths, along with cutting-edge gaming gear and technology.

CLOUD GAMING

Cloud gaming is changing the way video games are played. In cloud gaming, a remote server hosts the game. Players log on to the server instead of launching the game on their own consoles or computers. The player's controller inputs are sent to the server, and the game's video and audio are streamed back to the player. On a good internet connection, this process happens quickly enough to minimize the amount of lag. Cloud gaming offers people a way to play the latest games without having to buy an expensive new console or gaming PC.

This way, they can figure out what's hot, what's not, and what their players want.

The Tokyo Game Show in Japan is one annual gaming convention. The first day of the convention is for industry members only. It's a chance for game publishers and developers to hold meetings and network. Developers sit down for interviews and offer demos to journalists and reviewers. The general public is allowed to attend the next days of the convention.

Conventions can also be a valuable opportunity for players. They can be the first to try out new gaming gear, such as virtual reality headsets. Players can also test new games, talk to developers, and visit promotional booths run by Sony, Nintendo, and other major companies. People dreaming of jobs in the game industry can meet experienced professionals, make contacts, and learn more about the industry.

At the 2022 Tokyo Game Show, players could see levels from Quantic Dream's new project, *Star Wars Eclipse*. Quantic Dream specializes in reactive storytelling. This modern gaming trend allows players' choices to affect the storyline as the game moves forward. Gamers can also play as different characters. One choice in the game may lead to a

Developer Quantic Dream uses technology such as photogrammetry. During this process, dozens of cameras scan an actor or object from all angles. The scans are used to create a realistic, detailed 3D model.

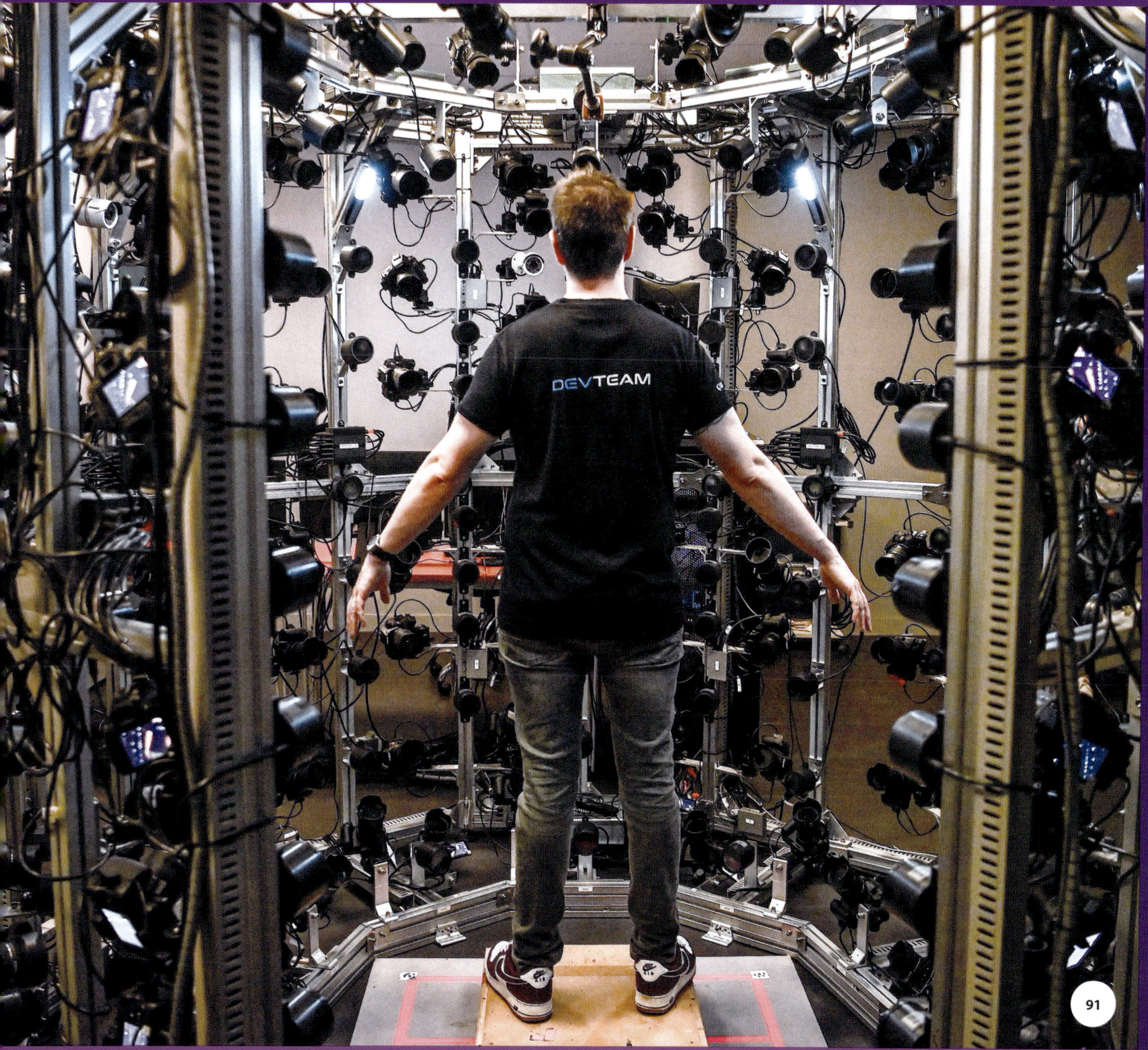
DEVTEAM

dangerous, difficult, and action-packed shootout. Another may plunge the player into a tense, dialogue-driven storyline.

For game developers, reactive storytelling offers a chance to bring new elements to their games—chance and randomness. But it requires a lot of work and writing. Each alternative storyline must be completely worked out. Some players may never even encounter some of the storylines when they play the game. The upside to reactive storytelling is that each time the game is played, it becomes something different. This keeps players involved with a game for longer periods of time.

DEVELOPING VR GAMES

Virtual reality (VR) technology has changed how people experience video games. As technology advances and becomes more affordable, this way of playing games may become more mainstream. VR headsets such as the PlayStation VR2 or Meta Quest 3 allow gamers to be surrounded by game environments, rather than players looking at them on a flat screen. This means games can have a much greater visual impact. Immersive horror games can frighten gamers with jump scares from the front, side, or back. Shooting games can require players to physically turn their bodies to aim in all directions.

But VR developers can't simply copy flat-screen video games to the VR headset. Some aspects of VR make traditional gameplay difficult or impossible. For example, a combo

VR headsets use motion-tracking technology and high-tech cameras to make players feel as though they're inside of a 3D game environment. Many sets come with handheld controllers.

fighting move in an environment that surrounds the player is tough to pull off. Cinematic cutscenes don't work well in VR, either. Stopping the gameplay to run a cutscene can be jarring for the player.

VR gamers also move more slowly through the game. Because there's more visual information in the game, they often pause or slow down to take it all in. Having more than one enemy to shoot at is also a challenge—VR players can aim only as fast as they can move their heads right or left. For VR fighting scenes, game designers must take this into account. The designer must also avoid overwhelming the player with fast motion or too much detail. VR players don't have real-world objects, such as tabletops, in view to steady themselves. As a result, they can develop motion sickness when wearing VR headsets. Game developers may need to conduct testing to prevent these reactions.

> **"It's very difficult to determine what is a should and a shouldn't in VR. I think the only rule is that there isn't any yet. . . . Not only is [VR] a different way of perceiving the world, it's a different way of being present in that world.[1]"**
>
> ***—Nick Witsel, game designer at Vertigo Games***

THE AI REVOLUTION

Artificial intelligence (AI) will also change the video game landscape. Generative AI is a computer algorithm or model that "studies" data inputted to it. When given a prompt, the model uses that data as examples in order to create new things, such as images or text, that are similar to those examples. This could take many routine development tasks off the shoulders of humans. In theory, generative AI can create stories, write dialogue, and generate scripts for cutscenes. Promethean AI is a tool that can create environments based on a certain time period or style. This technology allows the game developer or player to choose a game's environment. In one game, the tool built a world in the style of the TV show *Stranger Things* in just 15 minutes.[2]

Some future video games may be entirely produced by AI, with humans simply inputting a framework, story idea, or genre and then guiding the software as it works. Within games, "enemy AI" will also get smarter. Games have had this ability since the early 2000s, enabling non-player characters to predict a player's moves and change their actions accordingly. But future games could take this element of AI to new extremes.

ROBLOX

***Roblox* was one of the earliest and most successful independent games. By the summer of 2023, it had grown into a massive multi-world platform with more than 200 million active users.[3] It had also expanded into more than a game. In the *Roblox* metaverse, developers can market and sell their creations to a large audience of potential buyers. Players of all experience levels can also use the game engine Roblox Studio to make their own games.**

AN EVER-CHANGING INDUSTRY

Today, the world of video game development continues to evolve. New technology and trends are shaping the future of video games. Many game developers are paying

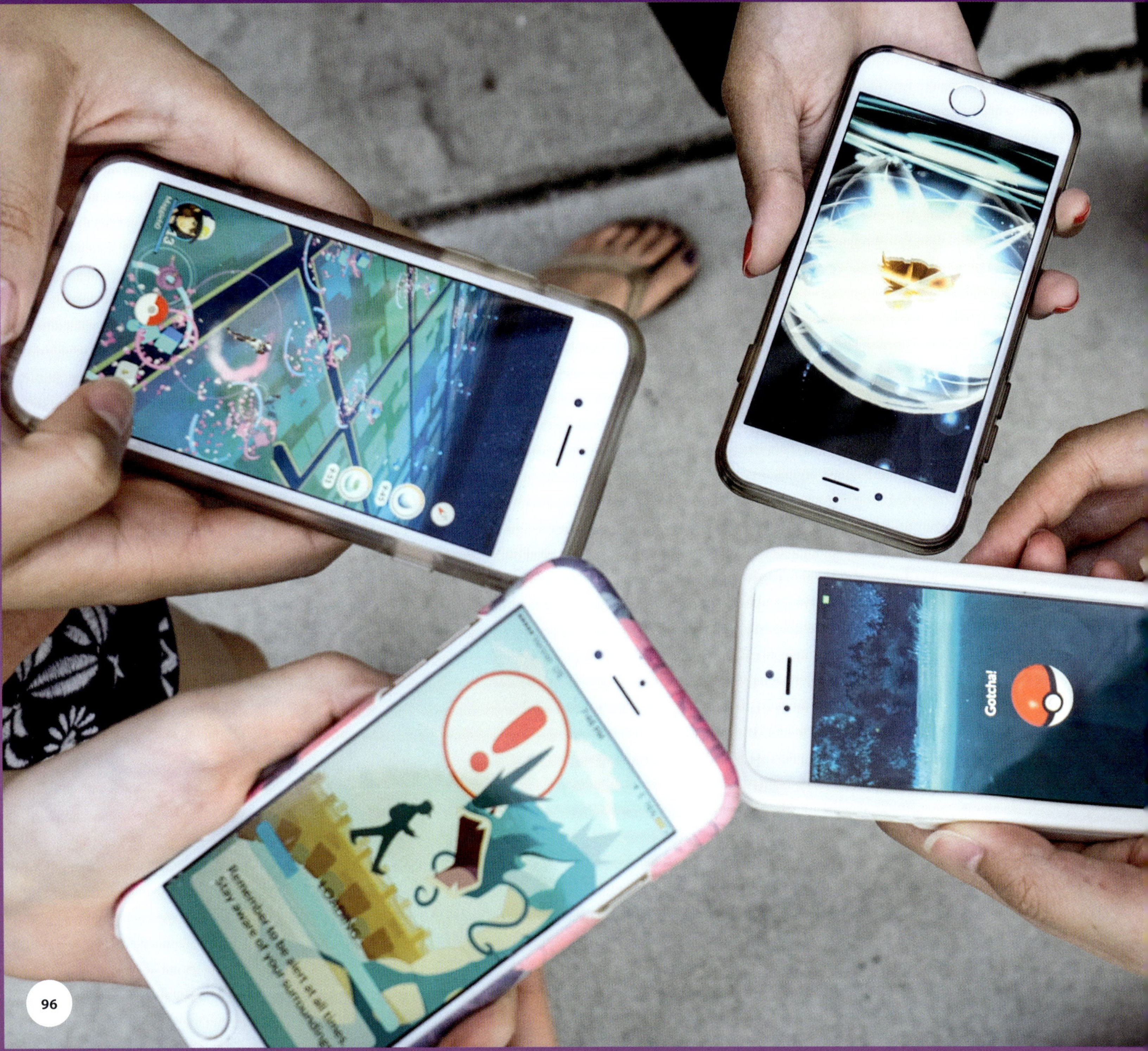
Gotcha!

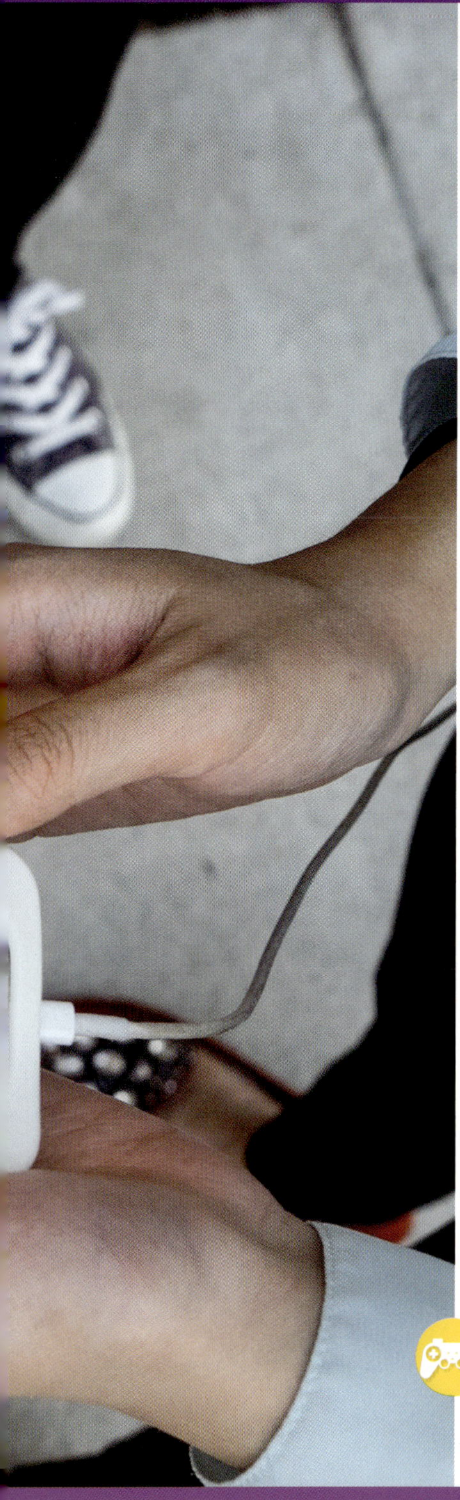

attention to the modern trend of retro gaming, or playing classic games from the past. Retro gaming has become very popular among players of all ages, even those too young to have played the original games. Millions of people play the earliest versions of *Halo, The Legend of Zelda,* and *Sonic the Hedgehog*. Some have gone all the way back to the arcade era with console versions of *Pac-Man* and *Donkey Kong*.

Publishers who own the rights to these games have put them back on the market. As new technology continues to develop, retro games will likely be incorporated into new, larger games. These games will challenge players even as they use new gaming technology such as VR headsets.

The mobile game *Pokémon Go* is a pioneer in another modern gaming trend, augmented reality (AR). In AR, the real world becomes a gamescape. Players go outside and are challenged to find places or things that exist in the real world. Other games have also embraced AR. The mobile fitness game *Zombies, Run!* involves audio narratives about escaping zombies. Players run or jog while listening to the game.

The popular game *Pokémon Go* encouraged millions of players to go outside and explore in search of Pokémon. The AR game uses GPS technology and digital camera overlays.

STEP ASIDE, STEAM

The business world has a phrase for companies that innovate successfully—first-mover advantage. This means a pioneer in a certain sector takes most or all of the market while others try to compete or catch up. Steam, for example, was the first big online game-selling platform, taking a majority of online game sales. But its first-mover advantage is now fading. There's itch.io for indie games, GOG.com for PC games, and Epic Games, which has the exclusive right to sell *Fortnite* content and in-game purchases. Gaming platforms such as PlayStation and Xbox have also begun to allow purchases and streaming. To keep up with the changing world of game development, Steam will have to innovate.

In *AR Sports Basketball,* gamers shoot hoops and make passes anywhere they want, with the app in hand. AR could change not only the world of gaming but also the world of work and business.

The range of new abilities in gaming technology will likely pose challenges for developers. "Adaptive difficulty" alters how hard a game is according to the player's success or failure. "Nondeterministic AI" changes outcomes and goals within a video game according to the player's in-game decisions. To use these features effectively, developers must use software tools to build decision trees, with certain outcomes matched to specific player actions and decisions.

AR, AI, and other new technologies will challenge video game developers to master knowledge as it is made available, rather than how it has already been taught. Books on programming will go out of date, and constantly updated websites on the topic will become a go-to source. For beginners in the business, classes and college degrees in programming and other game-related specialties may not be enough. Creators will likely need hands-on experience creating games to even break into the field.

Some companies offer immersive VR gaming experiences and arenas for groups of players.

Practicing game creation alone could become increasingly important. This means the competition for donations, downloads, and paid subscriptions will get even tougher. And as indie games draw bigger audiences, big-budget development companies may become a thing of the past. Although the demand for new video games is always strong, the technology and skills needed for success never stand still.

MAKING VIDEO GAMES PROFESSIONALLY

- Professional video game developers get funding for a game's production through a publisher. In some cases, the developer is owned by the publishing company.
- The first stage in the process is preproduction. During this stage, the game development team works up the game's concept, platform, genre, and storyline.
- A game development document (GDD) establishes a high-level view of the game's levels, gameplay mechanics, story, and characters. It also provides a production timeline and budget for the project.
- During the production stage, artists complete the game's design and animation. Programmers write the game's code. The game also goes through testing.
- Postproduction involves marketing the completed game. After the game is released, the developer collects feedback to fix any technical issues. The developer also prepares patches or downloadable content for the game.

MAKING VIDEO GAMES INDEPENDENTLY

- Independent game creators decide which genre or type of game they want to make. They also select a platform for the game, such as mobile, console, or PC. The developer may partner with a commercial publisher or choose to work independently.
- Independent developers may use crowdfunding or other methods to raise money for the game's development.
- Working on their own or with a small team, the developer designs the game's characters and art. They create the game's story and write its levels. Each team member may take on multiple roles in development.
- Releasing game demos, showcasing games at conventions, and inexpensive marketing campaigns on social media offer independent developers ways to promote their new releases.

QUOTE

"You can make an amazing game, but you can't make a success. Your players make the success."

—Imre Jele, cofounder of Bossa Games

GLOSSARY

artificial intelligence (AI)
The science of developing computers or technology that can think and act like humans. In video games, AI refers to the capacity of a video game to respond and adapt to its players.

augmented reality (AR)
The technique of combining computer-generated graphics or sound with the real world.

bug
A fault in the software code that causes problems or crashes in a video game.

console
An electronic hardware device that runs video games.

cutscene
A non-interactive cinematic scene that plays out during a video game.

debug
To correct errors in the programming code that are causing performance problems in a game.

game engine
A software package of various tools, settings, and functions that help simplify the process of building video games.

monetize
To use something to make money or to earn money from something.

open-source
Of or relating to computer software that is freely available to use, study, edit, and modify.

platform
The system or device on which a game runs, such as a console, handheld device, or personal computer. Also, a site or app used to publish, buy, sell, and download games.

port
To convert a video game designed for one platform so that it can be played on another platform.

user interface (UI)
The on-screen menus and graphics that players use to select characters, weapons, levels, and other game aspects under their control.

virtual reality (VR)
A computer-generated simulation of a three-dimensional environment.

SELECTED BIBLIOGRAPHY

Abramson, S. E. *The Secret Lives of Video Games*. Bushel and Peck, 2022.

Dille, Flint. *The Ultimate Guide to Video Game Writing and Design*. Watson-Guptill, 2007.

Schreier, Jason. *Blood, Sweat, and Pixels*. HarperCollins, 2017.

FURTHER READINGS

Jaskulka, Marie. *Making Web Content.* Abdo, 2025.

Kenney, Mary. *Gamer Girls*. Running, 2022.

Wheeler, Jill C. *Microsoft: Makers of the Xbox and* Minecraft. Abdo, 2023.

ONLINE RESOURCES

Booklinks
NONFICTION NETWORK
FREE! ONLINE NONFICTION RESOURCES

To learn more about making video games, please visit **abdobooklinks.com** or scan this QR code. These links are routinely monitored and updated to provide the most current information available.

MORE INFORMATION

For more information on this subject, contact or visit the following organizations:

DigiPen Institute of Technology
9931 Willows Rd. NE
Redmond, WA 98052
digipen.edu
Founded in 1988, DigiPen was the first school to offer degrees in video game technology and development. Students can earn bachelor's degrees and master's degrees.

Gameheads
2781 Telegraph Ave.
Oakland, CA 94612
gameheadsoakland.org
Gameheads is a technology training organization that prepares low-income youth in the San Francisco Bay area for careers in game design and development. Students learn how to code, manage workflows, work in teams, and complete interactive and multimedia projects.

National Videogame Museum
8004 Dallas Pkwy., Ste. 300
Frisco, TX 75034
nvmusa.org
The National Videogame Museum gives visitors a thorough history of the most popular creative medium in the world. It offers a huge collection of playable video games dating back to the 1970s and 1980s.

SOURCE NOTES

CHAPTER 1. VIDEO GAME ASSIGNMENT

1. Cassidee Moser. "Miyamoto Shares His Thoughts on Cinematic Games, Nintendo's Strategy." *IGN*, 17 Nov. 2014, ign.com. Accessed 1 Dec. 2023.

CHAPTER 2. THE HISTORY OF VIDEO GAMES

1. Geoff Brumfiel. "Total Failure: The World's Worst Video Game." *NPR*, 31 May 2017, npr.org. Accessed 1 Dec. 2023.

2. Scott Stilphen. "Howard Scott Warshaw Interview." *Atari Compendium*, n.d., ataricompendium.com. Accessed 1 Dec. 2023.

3. Sanjay Madhav. *Game Programming Algorithms and Techniques*. Addison Wesley, 2014. 3.

4. Matt Leone. "*Final Fantasy 7*: An Oral History." *Polygon*, 9 Jan. 2017, polygon.com. Accessed 1 Dec. 2023.

5. Jeremy Reimer. "Cross-Platform Game Development and the Next Generation of Consoles." *Ars Technica*, 7 Nov. 2005, arstechnica.com. Accessed 1 Dec. 2023.

6. Logan Moore. "*Call of Duty* 2022's Massive Budget Reportedly Revealed." *ComicBook.com*, 8 Feb. 2022, comicbook.com. Accessed 1 Dec. 2023.

7. "*Call of Duty*: *Modern Warfare II*: The Next-Gen Tech Engine Inspiring a Vastly Advanced Game Performance." *Call of Duty*, 5 Dec. 2022, callofduty.com. Accessed 1 Dec. 2023.

8. Ethan Gach. "Leaked Xbox Boss Email Perfectly Explains Why Game Publishers Are Eating Themselves Alive." *Kotaku*, 22 Sept. 2023, kotaku.com. Accessed 1 Dec. 2023.

CHAPTER 3. PREPRODUCTION FOR PROFESSIONAL GAMES

1. Nitin Garg. "AAA Game Development Cost: Everything You Need to Know." *BR Softech*, 7 June 2023, brsoftech.com. Accessed 1 Dec. 2023.

2. Tom Ivan. "Who Is Mark Cerny, the Man behind PS5?" *VGC*, 13 Feb. 2020, videogameschronicle.com. Accessed 1 Dec. 2023.

3. Jef Rouner. "Most Major Video Games Will Now Cost $70. No Thanks." *Datebook*, 21 Jan. 2021, datebook.sfchronicle.com. Accessed 1 Dec. 2023.

4. "How Does *Fortnite* Make Money?" *Back to Front Show*, n.d., backtofrontshow.com. Accessed 1 Dec. 2023.

CHAPTER 4. PRODUCING PROFESSIONAL GAMES

1. Mireia Fernández. "Code by the Numbers: How Many Lines of Code in Popular Programs, Apps, and Video Games?" *Softonic,* 23 Apr. 2023, en.softonic.com. Accessed 1 Dec. 2023.

2. Patches Chance. "How Long Did It Take to Make *GTA 5*?" *Outsider Gaming*, 30 Sept. 2023, outsidergaming.com. Accessed 1 Dec. 2023.

3. Natalie Flores. "Rockstar Games Reveals Details of *Red Dead Redemption 2*'s Development, Including 100-Hour Developer Work Weeks." *Paste*, 15 Oct. 2018, pastemagazine.com. Accessed 1 Dec. 2023.

4. "Video Game Designer Profile." *All Art Schools*, n.d., allartschools.com. Accessed 1 Dec. 2023.

CHAPTER 5. POSTPRODUCTION FOR PROFESSIONAL GAMES

1. Tom Senior. "*Cyberpunk 2077*'s 2.0 Update Is So Good You Should Consider Restarting from Scratch." *Eurogamer*, 26 Sept. 2023, eurogamer.net. Accessed 4 Dec. 2023.

2. Werner Geyser. "5 Examples of Mobile Gaming Influencer Marketing Done Right." *Influencer Marketing Hub*, 26 Oct. 2023, influencermarketinghub.com. Accessed 4 Dec. 2023.

3. Gustaf Lundberg Toresson. "The New Face of the Gaming Influencer." *Forbes*, 1 June 2022, forbes.com. Accessed 4 Dec. 2023.

CHAPTER 6. MAKING INDIE VIDEO GAMES

1. "Corporate Bios." *Tetris*, n.d., tetris.com. Accessed 4 Dec. 2023.

2. Brianna Scott. "Encore: The Number of Black Video Game Developers Is Small, but Strong." *NPR*, 25 Mar. 2023, npr.org. Accessed 4 Dec. 2023.

3. Rebekah Valentine. "Finding Humanity in *An Airport for Aliens Currently Run by Dogs*." *Games Industry*, 13 May 2020, gamesindustry.biz. Accessed 4 Dec. 2023.

4. Chris Kerr. "'If You Can't Create Something That Stands Out, You're Already Dead,' Says Bossa's Imre Jele." *Pocket Gamer*, 23 Sept. 2014, pocketgamer.biz. Accessed 4 Dec. 2023.

5. "On Being a Video Game Developer Today–The Risks and Rewards." *IndieGameReviewer*, 4 May 2016, indiegamereviewer.com. Accessed 4 Dec. 2023.

6. Tony Moore. "Markus Persson." *Biography*, 13 Apr. 2021, biography.com. Accessed 4 Dec. 2023.

CHAPTER 7. MARKETING INDIE GAMES

1. "How Much Does It Cost to Market a Video Game?" *Main Leaf*, 16 Feb. 2023, mainleaf.com. Accessed 4 Dec. 2023.
2. "Indie Game Marketing: Small Budget, Big Results." *HackerNoon*, 26 May 2021, hackernoon.com. Accessed 4 Dec. 2023.
3. J. Clement. "Number of Mobile Game Users Worldwide from 2017 to 2027 (in Millions)." *Statista*, 15 Jan. 2024, statista.com. Accessed 15 Jan. 2024.
4. "Meet Our 2021 Entrepreneur of the Year: Lee Hutchinson (Double Eleven)." *Entrepreneurs' Forum*, 23 Sept. 2023, entrepreneursforum.net. Accessed 4 Dec. 2023.
5. "'If You Want to Attract Female Talent into Gamedev You Need Games Made by Women for Women.'" *Inlingo*, 9 Dec. 2020, inlingogames.com. Accessed 4 Dec. 2023.
6. Sam White. "Valley Forged: How One Man Made the Indie Video Game Sensation *Stardew Valley*." *GQ*, 20 Mar. 2018, gq.com. Accessed 4 Dec. 2023.

CHAPTER 8. THE FUTURE OF VIDEO GAMES

1. Marie Dealessandri. "The Best Practices and Design Principles of VR Development." *Games Industry*, 2 Apr. 2020, gamesindustry.biz. Accessed 4 Dec. 2023.
2. "AI and the Future of Gaming for Game Devs." *Inworld*, 24 Aug. 2023, inworld.ai. Accessed 4 Dec. 2023.
3. Josh Howarth. "7 Huge Gaming Industry Trends 2024–2027." *Exploding Topics*, 24 Nov. 2023, explodingtopics.com. Accessed 4 Dec. 2023.

INDEX

ABOUT THE **AUTHOR**

TOM STREISSGUTH

An editor, teacher, web designer, and author, Tom Streissguth has written more than 100 books for young readers, covering subject areas such as history, geography, current events, and media. In 2017, he founded the Archive of American Journalism to publish the hard-to-find writings of major American writers such as H. L. Mencken, Nellie Bly, Stephen Crane, and Ray Stannard Baker. Tom lives in the Twin Cities area of Minnesota with his wife and his daughter, Bailey. He enjoys movies, sporting events, cooking, and traveling to Thailand and other destinations. He collects antique Japanese woodblock prints and enjoys reading dusty old pulp fiction magazines.